Quick Guide Legal Best Practices for Founders in Germany

AF812393

Benedikt Quarch · Dennis Geissler ·
Philippa Peters

Quick Guide Legal Best Practices for Founders in Germany

How Start-Up Formation, Financing, and Structuring Works

Springer

Benedikt Quarch
Düsseldorf, Germany

Dennis Geissler
Frankfurt am Main, Germany

Philippa Peters
Munich, Germany

ISBN 978-3-658-47384-6 ISBN 978-3-658-47385-3 (eBook)
https://doi.org/10.1007/978-3-658-47385-3

Translation from the German language edition: "Quick Guide Legal Best Practices für Gründer:innen" by Benedikt Quarch et al., © Der/die Herausgeber bzw. der/die Autor(en), exklusiv lizenziert an Springer Fachmedien Wiesbaden GmbH, ein Teil von Springer Nature 2024. Published by Springer Fachmedien Wiesbaden. All Rights Reserved.

This book is a translation of the original German edition "Quick Guide Legal Best Practices für Gründer:innen" by Benedikt Quarch et al., published by Springer Fachmedien Wiesbaden GmbH in 2024. The translation was done with the help of an artificial intelligence machine translation tool. A subsequent human revision was done primarily in terms of content, so that the book will read stylistically differently from a conventional translation. Springer Nature works continuously to further the development of tools for the production of books and on the related technologies to support the authors.

© The Editor(s) (if applicable) and The Author(s), under exclusive license to Springer Fachmedien Wiesbaden GmbH, part of Springer Nature 2025

This work is subject to copyright. All rights are solely and exclusively licensed by the Publisher, whether the whole or part of the material is concerned, specifically the rights of translation, reprinting, reuse of illustrations, recitation, broadcasting, reproduction on microfilms or in any other physical way, and transmission or information storage and retrieval, electronic adaptation, computer software, or by similar or dissimilar methodology now known or hereafter developed.
The use of general descriptive names, registered names, trademarks, service marks, etc. in this publication does not imply, even in the absence of a specific statement, that such names are exempt from the relevant protective laws and regulations and therefore free for general use.
The publisher, the authors and the editors are safe to assume that the advice and information in this book are believed to be true and accurate at the date of publication. Neither the publisher nor the authors or the editors give a warranty, expressed or implied, with respect to the material contained herein or for any errors or omissions that may have been made. The publisher remains neutral with regard to jurisdictional claims in published maps and institutional affiliations.

This Springer imprint is published by the registered company Springer Fachmedien Wiesbaden GmbH, part of Springer Nature.
The registered company address is: Abraham-Lincoln-Str. 46, 65189 Wiesbaden, Germany

If disposing of this product, please recycle the paper.

Contents

Business Idea 1

Founding 5

a. Choosing the Right Legal Form for You 6

aa) Partnership vs. Corporation 7

bb) Often Irrelevant Legal Forms 9

cc) GmbH 10

dd) UG (Limited Liability) 13

ee) GbR 13

ff) Current Adjustments, Especially the Introduction of the eGbR 15

b. Necessary Documents 15

Financing 17

a. Strategic Decisions 17

aa) Bootstrapping vs. External Capital 17

bb) Bootstrapping—Your most Important Facts 18

b. External Capital 19

c. Difference between Angels and VC 21

d. The Convertible Loan 21

e. Pooling of Angels 23
aa) Voting Pool 23
bb) Trust Solution 24
cc) Pool Companies 25
dd) UG (limited liability) or GmbH 26
ee) GmbH & Co. KG 26
ff) GbR 26
f. Summary of Advantages and Disadvantages of Pooling Solutions 27
g. Financing Round with a VC 28
aa) Term Sheet—what is it and what should it contain? 28
bb) VSOP: Who Gives Up Shares? 29
cc) Financing Tied to Milestones 29
dd) Liquidation Preferences 29
ee) Sample Documentation for a Financing Round (GESSI) 30
ff) Documents typically required for a VC financing round 30
gg) Due Diligence 31
h. Debt Financing 32
aa) Bank Loans 32
bb) Venture Debt 32
cc) Bonds 33

Staff 35
a. Staff Recruitment 35
b. Employment Contracts 37
aa) Designation 39
bb) Start and Duration 39
cc) Main Area of Activity 40
dd) Working Hours 40
ee) Remuneration 40
ff) Vacation 41
gg) Secondary Activities and Non-Competition Clause 41
hh) Confidentiality Agreement 41

c. Central Labor Law Provisions 42
aa) Initiation and Establishment of the Employment Relationship 42
bb) Obligations and Rights Arising from the Employment Relationship 43
cc) Termination of Employment 45
d. ESOP Employee Participation 47

Rules of Procedure for the Management 49
a. Process Flow—Communication, Decision and Filing 50
b. Typical Transactions Requiring Approval 51
c. Atypical Transactions Requiring Approval 52
d. Sample of Rules of Procedure 53
e. Approval Reservations for Management 55
aa) Statutory Provision in a GmbH 55
bb) Catalog of Transactions Requiring Approval 56

Investor Relations 57
a. Shareholder Rights According to the GmbH Act 57
b. In Practice: Monthly Reportings 59
c. Board Management 60

Good Governance for Managing Directors 61
a. Convening Ordinary/Extraordinary Shareholders' Meeting 61
b. Obligation to Deposit Balance Sheet and Accounting 62
c. Preparation of Tax Returns 62
d. Tax Registrations 62
e. Obligation to Maintain Share Capital 63
f. Obligation to File for Insolvency and Prohibition of Payments 63
aa) Obligation to File for Insolvency 64
bb) Prohibition of Payments 64
g. Legal Basis for Personal Liability 65

Helpful Tools 73
a. Fides (www.fides.technology) 73
b. Bunch (www.bunch.capital) 73
c. Ledgy (www.ledgy.com) and Carta (www.carta.com) 74

Protective Rights 75
a. Patents 75
b. Trademark 76
c. Copyright 77
d. Imitation Protection 77

General Terms and Conditions 79

Websites 81

Founders' Exit 85
a. Design Options 86
aa) Acquisition or Complete Sale to Strategic Investors 86
bb) Trade Sale and Private Equity 86
cc) Leveraged Buyout (LBO) 86
dd) IPO: Going Public 87
ee) Merger: Exit through Consolidation 87
ff) Timing 87
b. Typical Contract Components 88
aa) Purchase Price and Payment Modalities 88
bb) Warranties and Guarantees 88
cc) Non-Compete Clauses 89
dd) Restrictions on Disposal 89
ee) Transition Agreements 89
ff) Limitations of Liability 89
gg) Approval Requirements and Release Mechanisms 89

Worst-Case Scenario/Exit Strategy/Dispute Among Shareholders 91
a. Liquidation vs. Insolvency 92
b. Liability Risks in Insolvency 94
c. Dispute among the Shareholders 95

About the Authors

Dr. Benedikt Quarch is an entrepreneur and lawyer. He studied law and business administration in Wiesbaden and Montréal. For his achievements in the first state law examination, the Minister of Justice of the state of Hesse awarded him as the best graduate of the year 2016. In 2019, he received his doctorate from the EBS Law School, Wiesbaden. Since 2017, Benedikt Quarch has been the co-founder and managing director of the LegalTech company RightNow. In addition, Benedikt Quarch, who was named one of Forbes "30 under 30" in 2020 and one of "JUVE 40 under 40" in 2023, is the founder of the "Founders in Law" initiative, author of various legal textbooks, editor of the LegalTech Journal (LTZ) published by Nomos-Verlag, a business angel, and a postdoctoral researcher at the University of Cologne.

Philippa Peters is a lawyer and founder and COO/CLO of Fides—a LegalTech software company that enables companies to digitize, centralize, and automate their corporate governance workflows worldwide. Philippa Peters is also committed to the board of the Legal Tech Association of Germany. Previously, Philippa specialized as a lawyer in renowned law firms such as Noerr and Freshfields in corporate and insolvency law.

Dr. Dennis Geissler is a lawyer in Frankfurt am Main and a partner of the law firm "Ferox Legal". The firm primarily handles corporate law disputes (shareholder disputes, managing director and board liability, and post-M disputes). Previously, he was a partner in a larger, internationally oriented law firm. His clients include, among others, private equity funds, as well as founders and business leaders, whom he particularly supports in crisis scenarios. In addition, he is a start-up investor himself and has been involved in the establishment of many start-ups and subsequent exits. At the time of publication of this work, Dr. Dennis Geissler is active in various associations, including the Association of Family Entrepreneurs e. V.

Business Idea

Every company's story begins with a promising business idea. This involves a specific product or service that one intends to bring to the market and trade in the future.

After developing such an idea, the market environment must be analyzed. Of course, the approach to market placement can vary depending on the product. After all, we don't want to compare apples with pears. So let's assume that you want to trade lemons in the future. For this, you need to know exactly who your suppliers are and which customer base you want to target. You should also think about where you can sell your lemons and how you can get them from A to B most efficiently. Furthermore, you need to consider how profitable the market is, i.e., what markup can be expected when you buy the lemons and sell them again. This is technically called the theoretical selling price.

In the next step, your competition must be taken into account. So you ask yourself who else is operating in the lemon trade market and whether this is a large corporation with great market power or if there is a market gap in your case. For this, you need to differentiate between two types of products: The Me-too product, which describes a product that already exists on the market and of which you offer another variant,

© The Author(s), under exclusive license to Springer Fachmedien Wiesbaden GmbH, part of Springer Nature 2025

B. Quarch et al., *Quick Guide Legal Best Practices for Founders in Germany*, https://doi.org/10.1007/978-3-658-47385-3_1

and the USP product, which describes a completely new product and, for example, can represent a mix/cross between a lemon and an orange. Such a product does not yet exist on the market, is therefore unique, and is technically called a unique selling proposition. A product newly introduced to the market is in most cases much more promising than a simple Me-too product that already exists in a similar form.

The fundamental question to be noted is: What are you selling to whom, at what price, and how?

So once you have determined what you want to sell, i.e., developed the specific business idea, you move from your basic idea to detailed planning. The basis for this is the marketing mix. This in turn consists of the product, distribution, pricing policy, and communication mix.

The product describes, among other things, the business idea already explained. Furthermore, certain equipment elements are included. In this case, quality is particularly important. For your lemons, for example, you would only offer premium quality (edible peel, organic quality, etc.). Other components of the equipment elements would be customer service, quantity, design, and packaging. All these factors ultimately make up your final product.

Next to be included in your planning is the distribution mix, which is a synonym for the sales or distribution channel. So you should ask yourself how you want to sell your product. For lemons, selling through food retail, fruit shops, discounters, or even the internet is an option. For other products, specialty stores might be an option. In principle, you could sell your product directly from the manufacturers to the end customers or via B2B (business to business) to resellers.

Another fundamental question concerns the concept of pricing policy. You need to be clear about how expensive you can offer your product to remain profitable. Setting a goal for a lemon to be the most expensive lemon in the world, for example, would not be very lucrative, as consumers are unlikely to accept a high price for lemons.

As a final step, you should deal with the communication mix. This includes the question of what form of advertising or public relations should be used.

After you have thought through this step and included it in your planning, you can check off the first item on your to-do list. The basic settings to place your product in the market are in place.

But one crucial component is still missing: What are the legal foundations of starting a business? That's what this book is about.

Founding

After we have explained and internalized the development of the essential business idea, we now continue with the establishment of your future company.

For this, it is first necessary that you familiarize yourself with the various forms of companies, despite the *numerus clausus* applicable in corporate law. You should proceed quite carefully in this regard. A product alone is not enough to run a lucrative business. Rather, it is about protecting yourself in this step. After all, you need a certain limitation of liability, otherwise the entire financial risk could hit you. In the event that you suffer a shipwreck with your product, you are faced with a pile of rubble that you can control or limit through the right form of company.

However, when determining the form of company, you do not have to be hesitant or even unsure. The decision about your chosen legal form is not final, but is reviewed at regular intervals after successful establishment. If the framework conditions undergo a change, an adjustment can be made.

© The Author(s), under exclusive license to Springer Fachmedien Wiesbaden GmbH, part of Springer Nature 2025

B. Quarch et al., *Quick Guide Legal Best Practices for Founders in Germany*, https://doi.org/10.1007/978-3-658-47385-3_2

a. Choosing the Right Legal Form for You

Giving a blanket answer as to which legal form you should choose for your start-up is difficult and depends on many individual factors. Accordingly, it is up to you to first define the purpose and objectives of your start-up. In a further step, it then requires a confrontation with the personal circumstances of all participants, how they relate to each other and a comprehensive inventory of the circumstances affecting the company. This can generally be divided into personal and economic factors. Keep in mind that the procedure described below is not exhaustive. The basic rule is to identify those factors in the search for the right form of company that are suitable for reflecting the interests of the participants.

The personal factors include individual goals of all participants, which are pursued with the establishment of the start-up. To specify this, the respective professional and technical backgrounds (especially possible, relevant licenses) are important. In a further step, it is necessary to determine the capital provided by the participants and their labor input. It is particularly important here to establish the hierarchy planned in the company in order to create clear positions, tasks, and rights vis-à-vis others. In a final step, you should illuminate legal issues, especially the willingness to assume liability. For this, it is necessary to explain the legal basics of your chosen form of company to each participant precisely to prevent misunderstandings later. After you have discussed all these raised questions, you can tick off the personal factors.

Then you should turn to the economic factors. There is a slight overlap with the personal factors here, as the question is raised as to how much capital is available to the start-up and especially where it comes from. Note that the following criteria can often coincide and the list is not exhaustive:

1. Financing taking into account ongoing taxation
2. Remuneration to entrepreneurs
3. Limitation of liability and disclosure obligation
4. Management, supervision, co-determination
5. Group of companies

6. Company purchase, sale
7. Real estate in company assets
8. Company succession
9. Conversion
10. Founding expenses
11. International aspects

After successfully completing this checklist, some types of companies should already be eliminated from your decision-making process. For the remaining legal forms, you should assign individual weights to the respective advantages and disadvantages in a further step. Of course, you should be aware that compromises are typically unavoidable. However, it should be noted in any case that your choice of law could be partially restricted by law. This could result from the purpose of the company itself or from the structure of the shareholders, although for a large part of start-ups, the company purposes affected by these restrictions (including pharmacies, insurance companies or banking companies) are not relevant. Regarding the structure of the shareholders, it should be noted that certain legal forms, such as the GbR or OHG, cannot be chosen when founding a start-up by a single person. In contrast, the establishment of a GmbH as a one-person company is possible.

The following will present the individual types of companies. This initially requires a distinction between the partnership and the corporation. Subsequently, the focus will be on the GmbH/UG and the GbR, which are considered the most relevant legal forms for start-ups.

aa) Partnership vs. Corporation

The first thing you should consider in the context of types of companies is the fundamental distinction between a partnership and a corporation, which affects internal and external relations, but can be limited in practice by the design of the partnership agreements. Furthermore, there are so-called hybrid forms, which also fall into the category of partnerships.

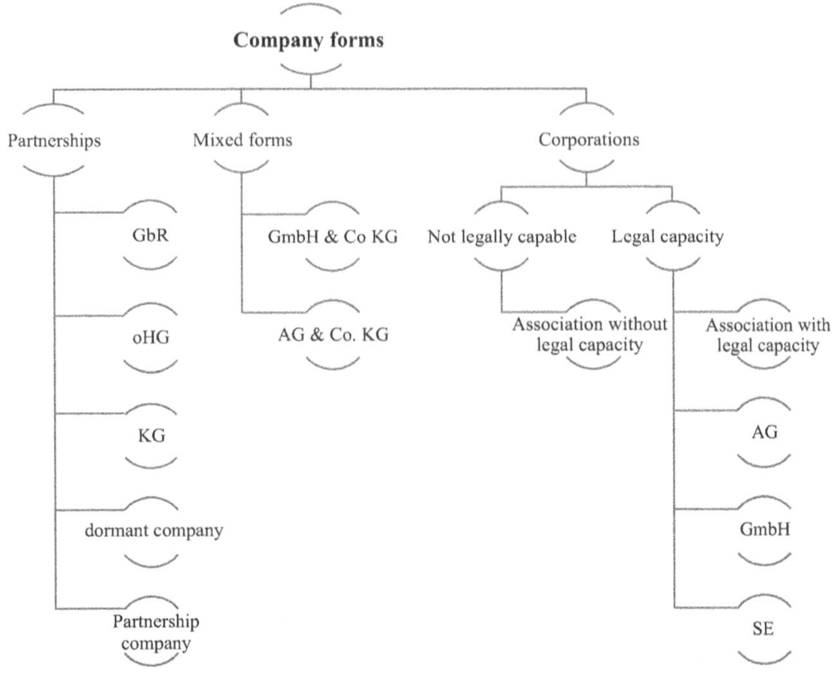

Partnerships: GbR, OHG, KG
Corporations: Association, GmbH/UG, AG, SE
Hybrid forms (part of the partnerships): GmbH/UG & Co. KG, AG & Co. KG, GmbH & Co. KGaA, GmbH & Silent, Partnership Company (PartG/PartGmbB)

To get a precise idea of partnerships, we will now go into more detail on this.

Their legal basic form is the civil law partnership (GbR), which finds its regulations in the §§ 705 ff. BGB and is considered the most relevant partnership in the context of company formation. Basically, the partnership is only a somewhat independent association of persons towards its members.

Partnerships are characterized by the following key principles:

1. Smaller number of members, based on personal trust
2. Basic dissolution of the company when partners leave, §§ 723 ff. BGB
3. Usually all partners act together as managers/representatives (§ 715 BGB)
4. Principle of self-organ (only partners can act as managers/ representatives)
5. Basically informal contract conclusion between the members during the formation
6. Direct external liability (partners are generally directly liable with their private assets for company liabilities, cf. § 721 BGB)
7. Transfer of shares generally not provided for (cf. § 711 BGB), but possible with unanimity or corresponding regulation in the partnership agreement

The legal basic forms of corporations are in particular the GmbH and the UG. Basically, the corporation is an independent association person towards its members. Below you will find a further list of key principles that characterize corporations:

1. The existence is independent of a change of members
2. Majority principle (exception: amendment of the articles of association, regularly ¾ majority required)
3. Third-party organ (managers and representatives do not have to be company members)
4. Registration system (in addition to contract conclusion, registration in a register is generally required)
5. Shareholders only owe their contribution in the internal relationship (there is generally no liability beyond this towards third parties)

bb) Often Irrelevant Legal Forms

Before we delve further into the GmbH/UG and the GbR, it should be briefly explained at this point which legal form is rather to be rejected for business formation.

This is firstly the stock corporation (AG), which you are probably already familiar with. Basically, only rather large companies with a founding capital of at least €50,000 use this legal form. The share capital is broken down into shares. The disadvantages of this legal form are particularly found in the complex planning, financing, formation, and organization of the same. Furthermore, double-entry bookkeeping is required as well as a starting capital of at least €50,000. Another disadvantage is the fact that at least three founders are required for formation, a supervisory board must be appointed, and there is limited room for maneuver, as a strict legal framework exists. Overall, no recommendation can be made for business formation via a stock corporation.

Another—rather rarely used—legal form for the formation of start-ups is the Private Limited Company by Shares (Ltd.). What at first glance appears to many founders as a secret weapon (no personal liability, minimal equity, supposed protection from warnings due to location abroad, tax advantages of a corporation, low bureaucratic effort in the formation, low liability capital) however, also has a downside. This legal form does not protect against warnings. Furthermore, numerous legal questions, such as the question of personal (piercing) liability, are unresolved. The Ltd. as such is generally not well regarded by most entrepreneurs. In addition, a company address and a representative in England are usually required. If the main activity is in Germany, German insolvency law is applied and both legal systems (the German and the English legal system) must always be considered.

cc) GmbH

The most widespread legal form in Germany is the GmbH, which as of 01.01.2017 was estimated at a number of 1.22 million in the Federal Republic (*Kornblum*, Nationwide legal facts on corporate and company law (as of 1.1.2017), GmbHR 2017, 739).

As a corporation, it is a separate legal entity (§ 13 para. 1 GmbHG), which exists autonomously from the shareholders. By applying relevant transformation laws, the GmbH can also be merged with other legal forms, change its legal form, or be split into other legal forms, for which there are no further restrictions.

Due to its popularity, the GmbH will be examined in more detail below. In this context, we want to focus on the formation, liability, structure, and taxation.

The formation of the GmbH is not fundamentally limited to specific purposes (§ 1 GmbHG) and is carried out by one or more natural or legal persons (§ 1 GmbHG) based on an underlying partnership agreement, which must be notarized. Such a contract must name the company, location and object, share capital and amount of the share contribution. The minimum share capital of a GmbH is subject to a value of at least €25,000. At the time of the company's formation, it is necessary to pay in at least half of the share contribution (at least €12,500). The admission of new members is either through a transfer of shares from old shareholders or a capital increase by issuing new shares. Note that the company can establish contractual restrictions regarding the transfer.

With regard to the basic liability of the GmbH, you should note that the company form has its own assets, with which it is liable and which is composed of the contributions of the shareholders (§ 13 para. 2 GmbHG). A further personal liability with private assets is generally not applicable, provided that the participants in the partnership agreement have not agreed to a (un)limited additional obligation (§§ 26-28 GmbHG), which obliges them to comply with corresponding requirements, and the members have provided their respective company share (§ 27 GmbHG). On the other hand, there must be no loans granted to the company by the participants, as these cannot be reclaimed in a crisis.

The most important position within the company is the position of the managing directors. These can generally be freely chosen within a GmbH and do not necessarily have to be shareholders (principle of external directorship, § 6 para. 2 GmbHG). The number of managing directors, whether only one person alone or several jointly, is also freely selectable (§ 6 para. 1 GmbHG). Their task is typically to manage the business internally and represent the company externally. The law assumes the principle of overall management and representation (§§ 35, 36 GmbH), which is often modified in practice.

Another organ of the GmbH is the shareholders' meeting. This makes the decisions assigned to it by law and by the articles of association. Typically, these are fundamental decisions, such as the amendment of the articles of association, the appointment/dismissal of managing directors, or the dissolution of the company. Under certain circumstances, the GmbH may also be obliged to establish bodies such as a supervisory board or advisory board. This is particularly the case when it comes to fulfilling the Works Constitution Act or the Co-Determination Act.

By being equipped with its own legal personality, profits and losses of the GmbH from its activities are determined, which are subject to taxation. The shareholders then have a claim to the annual surplus or balance sheet profit, provided that these are prepared taking into account the use of the result (§ 29 para. 1 GmbHG). In the resolution on the use of the result, the participants can, if the articles of association do not specify otherwise, then set aside amounts in retained earnings or possibly carry them forward as profit (§ 29 para. 2 GmbHG). Distribution is made according to the ratio of the business shares, although a different scale of distribution can be set in the articles of association (§ 29 para. 3 GmbHG). In addition, interim payments can be made to the members, which, however, must represent advance payments on the expected profit. In the event of a lower profit being generated, overpayments are refunded to the company. As a form merchant, the legal form is subject to the general accounting and valuation regulations of §§ 238 to 263 HGB. In addition, supplementary regulations for corporations according to §§ 264 ff. HGB are to be used, which determine an extended annual financial statement by preparing an annex and a management report.

Due to the legal independence of the GmbH, the participants can enter and leave the legal form without affecting their existence. A change of shareholders thus only takes place at the level of the members by transferring the share in the company, which in turn must be notarized.

dd) UG (Limited Liability)

A subgroup of the GmbH is the UG (entrepreneurial company), which does not embody its own legal form.

The reason for the creation of the UG are legal policy considerations. The GmbH was in competition with other European forms of company (especially the already mentioned Limited), which often had significantly more favorable founding conditions. The UG can only be created by foundation, a "downgrading" of a GmbH to a UG is excluded. The required share capital, excluding contributions in kind, must be provided before registration.

The regulations of the GmbH apply in principle to the UG, unless § 5a GmbHG stipulates otherwise. However, the participants may be given the opportunity to bring about the limitation of liability by a lower share capital than €25,000, provided the company is referred to as "entrepreneurial company (limited liability)" (§ 5a para. 1 GmbHG). Interestingly, a share capital of just €1 is sufficient! Until the amount of €25,000 is reached, a quarter of the annual profit must be retained in the years after the foundation. In the event of impending insolvency, a shareholders' meeting must be convened immediately (§ 5a para. 4 GmbHG).

ee) GbR

Our last company form to be examined is the previously mentioned GbR. It represents the basic form of a partnership and requires the achievement of a specific, unrestricted purpose (§ 705 BGB) for its establishment.

In external relations, the GbR is limitedly legally capable following a basic decision of the BGH (BGH, NJW 2001, 1056), which means it can potentially not only be a creditor and debtor of (contractual or statutory) claims, but also acquire property rights and own (movable and immovable) things. Moreover, it is capable of being a party itself and can therefore sue and be sued in a legal dispute.

It is interesting that the GbR can also be considered for the operation of a small business, provided that the nature and extent of the business activity do not require a commercially organized business operation (§ 1 para. 2 HGB), so that the operation of a commercial enterprise is also possible. It is important to understand at this point that the GbR cannot be attributed the characteristic of a merchant, as the legal form does not operate a commercially organized company in the sense of § 1 HGB.

Regarding the establishment of the GbR, form requirements are generally irrelevant for you. However, in individual cases, this may be subject to exceptions, for example, if the establishment is carried out with the contribution of land or company shares (§§ 311b BGB, 15 para. 3 GmbHG).

As a fundamental characteristic of partnerships, the GbR is also subject to the principle of self-organization. The management (internal relationship) and the representation of the legal form (external relationship) are exclusively carried out by the respective partners, whereby the principle of joint representation always applies (§ 715 BGB). However, note that in practice, for reasons of practicability, individual representation is often agreed (§§ 715 para. 4 BGB).

The assets of the GbR are generally separate from the assets of the participants. This therefore forms an independent company assets according to § 713 BGB, which is liable for all liabilities incurred in the name of the company and into which enforcement can also be carried out in the event of a corresponding conviction (§ 722 BGB). However, the principle of accessory liability of the partners also applies (§ 721 BGB). This means that the members are personally liable with their entire assets for the liabilities of the GbR in addition to the joint assets of the company.

Furthermore, the profit of the GbR, unless a different agreement has been made, is handled according to the agreed participation ratios (§ 709 para. 3 BGB). In the absence of contrary legal regulation, withdrawals can be made at any time.

Based on a resolution by the partners, new members can join the company and also leave. However, note that new entrants are always liable for liabilities established before their entry, i.e., old liabilities (§ 721a BGB). Such liability can also affect departing members. The prerequisite for this is that liabilities incurred before their departure exist and these become due within five years after the entry of the departure in the commercial register (§ 160 para. 1 sentence 1 HGB). The transformation into a corporation, on the other hand, is only possible through individual legal succession in the form of a transfer of the GbR's economic goods to a GmbH.

ff) Current Adjustments, Especially the Introduction of the eGbR

On January 1, 2024, the law on partnerships was comprehensively reformed. The most important innovation is the introduction of the eGbR, i.e., the (in the partnership register) registered GbR (see § 707 BGB). For the first time, the legislator expressly recognized the legal capacity of the GbR in this context. The eGbR facilitates, among other things, the transfer of ownership and enables easier registration in the land register. In addition, the internal relationship of the partners is modernized, with a focus on greater flexibility and clearer structures. The reforms aim to increase legal certainty and make the eGbR more attractive for smaller companies and professional partnerships.

b. Necessary Documents

In addition to determining the legal form of the company and its corresponding establishment, you usually have to register with the trade office. To properly register your start-up as a business, you need certain documents and records, which can vary depending on the type of business operation. An example is the trade license (§ 34c GewO). Activities in the fields of liberal professions, science, and the agriculture and forestry industry are exceptions and do not require registration.

When registering, you should have the following documents ready:

- Identity card or passport with registration certificate
- Application for business registration
- Commercial register extract (only for corporations or general partnerships)
- Residence permit (only for founders from abroad)

For businesses that require a license, the following documents may also become essential:

- Certificate of non-objection from the tax office
- Medical certificates from the public health department
- Restaurant license
- Police clearance certificate

Financing

a. Strategic Decisions

Unfortunately, a company cannot be built on air and love alone, in any case, you need the necessary financial resources. How much and from whom it should come varies with the question of what kind of company you want to build, how your current situation presents itself, which industry you are aiming for, and what your personal goals are.

aa) Bootstrapping vs. External Capital

You have probably already read many reports about startups that collect horrendous sums from investors and almost felt that this was the only way to build a successful startup. In this context, there is good news for you: This is by no means the case! Rather, there are countless prominent examples that have bootstrapped for a while and only later raised capital, such as Celonis. The company now embodies the most valuable startup in Germany and initially self-financed "bootstrapped" for five years from consulting projects. Thanks to bootstrapping, the founders

© The Author(s), under exclusive license to Springer Fachmedien Wiesbaden GmbH, part of Springer Nature 2025

B. Quarch et al., *Quick Guide Legal Best Practices for Founders in Germany*,
https://doi.org/10.1007/978-3-658-47385-3_3

still hold the majority, i.e., over 50% of their company and are each proud multi-billionaires.

(https://www.manager-magazin.de/unternehmen/tech/celonis-wie-deutschlands-wertvollstes-start-up-zum-konzern-werden-will-a-6d29def1-b876-422f-9d19-cdc7fa87fffe).

bb) Bootstrapping—Your most Important Facts

Bootstrapping by no means implies that you don't need any capital. Even in bootstrapped companies, the founders invest, but their own money, their working time, or the money earned from consulting projects. You can also speak of bootstrapping when funds in the five-figure range are invested in a "Friends & Family" round. In any case, you are considered a bootstrapped company as long as no institutional capital providers are brought on board or higher six-figure sums are accepted from private investors.

Your advantages regarding bootstrapping

- You do not give up shares or only at a later point in time, which are significantly lower compared to a surrender at the beginning of your company history.
- You are not obliged to report regularly to investors.
- There are no foreign voting rights regarding strategy and business as well as further approval requirements of your financiers.
- Your organic growth can be more sustainable than financed growth and prompts you to quickly find the product-market fit.

Your disadvantages regarding bootstrapping

- Due to the restrictive budgeting, you may not take the same risks.
- You have to expect fewer investments regarding your employees, tools, marketing, etc.

- There is increased pressure on you, as the founder's own work is the biggest lever to advance the company.
- You should expect that your company will grow more slowly and you will have to accept initially foregoing many conveniences, e.g., an appropriate salary for the founders.

For some business models, bootstrapping may not even be an option per se. This is fundamentally the case when high initial investments are necessary for you, e.g., because a product has to be developed for one to two years before customers and sales can be recorded, or if you, as a non-technical founder, commission the product development via an agency or external developers. Depending on how complex and elaborate your product is, this can incur costs of several hundred thousand euros. Bootstrapping also makes less sense if you are pursuing an asset-heavy business model and need, for example, a production hall, laboratory, etc.

In any case, even when bootstrapping, a capital company (see above UG, GmbH, etc.) should be founded so that you limit your personal liability.

b. External Capital

Nowadays, it is common for institutional investors to finance a founding team with their idea already in the so-called **Pre-Seed Phase**. Ideally, at this point, you can already demonstrate an MVP (Minimum Viable Product) or some other type of demand (e.g., first users, customer contracts, or Letters of Intent), although there are also cases where the team itself is convincing and thus the idea in the form of a pitch deck is persuasive in terms of an investment.

For many founders, it is attractive to get "VC Money" from investors early on, i.e., to get financed. Pre-Seed financing usually ranges from a few hundred thousand euros to one to two million euros. The start-up financing allows you to invest full throttle into the necessary resources to launch the company.

You receive the money from these investors in exchange for shares in the newly founded company. This is usually structured in the Pre-Seed Phase through a convertible loan or through direct participation as a shareholder.

Your advantages of external capital

- **Faster growth:** Access to external capital can allow your start-up to grow faster and make larger investments in marketing, development, and scaling.
- **Access to resources:** External investors can bring not only capital but also resources, networks, and expertise that can help your start-up in the development and implementation of its business strategy.
- **Risk sharing:** External investors bear a portion of the financial risk, which can give you a certain financial security.
- **Better equipment:** External financing can better equip your start-up to respond to market changes and compete against competitors.

Your disadvantages of external capital

- **Dilution of founder shares:** With each financing round, the investors receive new shares, which can lead to a gradual reduction of your ownership stake.
- **Dependence on investors:** A start-up reliant on external financing can be somewhat dependent on the expectations and requirements of the investors, which often leads to restrictions on entrepreneurial freedom.
- **High competition for capital:** The process of raising capital can be competitive and time-consuming, and not all start-ups are successful in attracting external investors.

c. Difference between Angels and VC

The beautiful English term "Angel Investor", or Angel for short, has also established itself in Germany and refers to a private individual who participates in a startup as a shareholder with their private assets. An Angel round is usually synonymous with the Pre-Seed round, i.e., the first external capital that flows in. In contrast, the VC round is relevant, where "VC" stands for Venture Capital, or risk capital. VCs are professional, institutional investors who typically invest larger sums than Angel investors. In addition to capital, VC investors often also offer strategic advice, industry expertise, and networking contacts to promote the growth and success of your company. On the investor side, it is clear that the risks in this form of investment are high, as many start-ups fail.

d. The Convertible Loan

In a pre-seed round, it is common to collect the first financing through a convertible loan. This has the advantage that you save yourself the trip to the notary, as you do not directly transfer business shares. But first, we should deal with what a convertible loan (or in English a "**Convertible Loan**") is.

A convertible loan is a special form of corporate financing in which an investor provides money in the form of a loan. The special feature: This loan is only converted into company shares at the time of the next financing round. Unlike traditional loans where you pay interest, the investor here has the option to convert the loan amount into company shares. This offers advantages for both sides: Investors get the chance to participate in the success of your company, and you as a founder receive urgently needed capital, which you do not have to repay in cash.

Your advantage of a convertible loan

- **Fast and unbureaucratic processing:** Since you do not go to the notary when concluding a convertible loan according to common practice, it is sufficient to sign the convertible loan agreement from both sides.

Your disadvantage of a convertible loan

- **Legal certainty:** Basically, according to the GmbHG, the transfer of GmbH shares requires the notarial form. If this is not adhered to, the contract is formally void. With a convertible loan, a contract for the transfer of shares is only indirectly concluded, but there are lawyers who believe that even with such an indirect transfer, a notarial form is necessary for the effectiveness of the contract. This sounds problematic at first, but in practice this legal uncertainty is usually ignored in favor of speed.

You can download a template for a convertible loan from the German Standard Settings Institute (GESSI) via this link https://standardsinstitute.de/standardvertraege/wandeldarlehen.

When designing a convertible loan, the following points are particularly important for you:

1. **Cap and Discount**
   Cap: The "**Valuation Cap**" means the valuation of the company at which the loan will be converted in the next financing round.
   Discount: The discount for the investor on the valuation of the next financing round (usually about 20–30 %).
   Both discount and cap can be agreed together in a convertible loan agreement. Then the loan converts at the lower valuation.
2. **Mandatory Conversion**
   Most angels will ensure that a mandatory conversion of the share in the convertible loan is agreed, even if no financing round has taken place within a certain period (for example one to two years).

3. **Subordination**
   A subordination will help you so that the convertible loan does not appear as "debts" on your balance sheet and you possibly slide into insolvency as a result. Make sure to have a "qualified subordination". It's best to ask a friendly lawyer about this to be on the safe side.

e. Pooling of Angels

If you collect money with your start-up over several rounds, the number of shareholders naturally increases. At a certain point, it becomes an insurmountable effort to chase the signatures of all shareholders for a simple shareholder resolution. The shareholder resolution for the determination of the annual financial statements can thus take months, as one or the other angel has absconded to Ibiza and does not check his mails during this time. Also, negotiating the next round becomes a nightmare when more than ten parties want to negotiate contracts. To prevent these scenarios, it is advisable to pool your shareholders as early as possible. Pooling means implementing mechanisms to reduce the number of voting parties. In practice, the angels are often pooled, as they usually hold the smallest share in the company.

Three different possibilities have been established for the pooling of angels: 1) The voting pool, 2) The trust solution, and 3) The founding of a pool company.

aa) Voting Pool

The simplest variant for you is the so-called voting pool, in which several shareholders internally agree to cast their votes uniformly according to the results of internal votes. Legally speaking, this means that the pooled angels appoint a pool leader and authorize them to vote on behalf of the pool externally, to represent it. This means that the entire pool votes with the same decision. However, this decision must first be determined by an internal decision within the pool. This in turn means that the administrative effort for this solution can still be relatively high.

Voting pools are very easy to implement, as it only requires a power of attorney from the pooled angels, but their use is often limited. On the one hand, the members remain direct shareholders of the company and as such are also listed in the commercial register and in the rubric of each shareholder agreement. As such, they are still free to behave externally as they wish, i.e., to vote contrary to the pool regulations.

Only in the internal relationship of the pool contract can they make themselves liable for damages, but this requires a specific identifiable damage. To reduce the risk of coordinated voting behavior, there are occasionally more or less hard powers of attorney for pool leaders, which are supposed to give them the immediate authority to act independently instead of the pool member.

bb) Trust Solution

Another possibility to pool angels is the so-called trust solution. In a trust solution, a trustee takes over the majority of the property rights of the trust assets (= shares of the company) from the economically entitled person (= the angel) in an administrative role and appears externally as the owner.

This requires a trust agreement, which must be notarized for GmbH shares and reported to the responsible tax offices. Bunch, a start-up (www.bunch.capital), has specialized in this solution and acts as a trustee for start-ups with a large number of angels.

The trust solution results in trustees appearing instead of the angels in your start-up's shareholder list. They replace the angel in all typical voting processes in the company, both in shareholder resolutions and processes according to the shareholder agreement.

If this trust is set up correctly, it can be tax-neutral. This means that in the event of a possible exit profit, which would first be paid out to the trustee, it can be passed on to the trustor in the internal relationship, i.e., without deducting a tax burden at this level. The trustor (= the angel) then has to tax the exit profit 1:1, as if they had been directly involved.

WARNING In the event that your angels have applied for the INVEST grant from BAFA, they will not be very happy about this solution. The INVEST grant requires that the funded angel holds his shares himself for at least three years. This would not be the case with the trust solution. This means that the angel would have to repay the INVEST grant. The trust solution and also the pool company would therefore only be possible after the angel has held his shares for three years. The only option to consider here is the voting pool.

In addition to the INVEST problem, the tax limits must also be observed. To maintain tax transparency, it is essential that the trust relationship is not too strongly designed. This in turn means that the angel retains sufficient rights to maintain the character of a company participation to a certain degree.

This character can be maintained by not completely decoupling the trustee's voting right externally from instructions from the trustor internally to the trustee. The trust agreement should therefore provide a mechanism with which the trustor is asked for a decision and thus instruction in internal voting decisions (as with the voting pool) before the trustee then votes externally. This execution of the instruction request should be sufficiently documented.

For the documentation of instruction requests and the execution of shareholder resolutions, Fides (www.fides.technology) has found a good solution. Fides offers you templates for these shareholder resolutions and instruction requests. You can automate the entire process of creating, voting, and documenting the results via Fides. This saves you the legal costs that you would otherwise have to spend on legally secure creation and documentation.

cc) Pool Companies

The premium solution for pooling is the establishment of a pool company. This is a company that holds the entire number of pooled shares in the start-up. The angels, in turn, hold shares in the pool company in proportion to their participation.

CAUTION The above applies to the pool company with regard to the INVEST grant.

Here, the pool company can of course also take any form of company. The choice of the respective form of company has its usual advantages and disadvantages:

dd) UG (limited liability) or GmbH

The UG or GmbH as a pool company are common for pooling about 10 parties. The disadvantage, however, is that in the event of an exit, under current legislation, an effective tax burden of approximately 1.5% would be incurred on the exit proceeds.

ee) GmbH & Co. KG

For larger pools, setting up a GmbH & Co. KG is advisable. The advantage of a GmbH & Co. KG is that the pool remains tax-transparent through a purely asset-managing KG, i.e., no taxation occurs at the level of the pool shareholders, but only at the level of the participating investors. Also, voting rights and decision-making processes can be regulated comprehensively and almost flexibly in the KG contract, unlike in the articles of association of the GmbH.

ff) GbR

A GbR can also act as a pool company. The advantages of the GbR are that the establishment and operation of a GbR are simpler and cheaper than with a GmbH. Furthermore, a GbR, like the KG, is tax-neutral. However, the associated disadvantages should not be overlooked:

On the one hand, all partners of a GbR are fully liable for all business of the GbR. Any partner in a GbR can terminate their participation. This inevitably leads to the question of how to deal with the other proportionally pooled shares in the start-up and thus the entire shareholder agreement framework.

In summary, setting up a pool company would only be advisable for you if there are many shareholders to be pooled, you have a person in the start-up who has the legal understanding to lead such a pool company, and you are sure that this has no tax disadvantages.

f. Summary of Advantages and Disadvantages of Pooling Solutions

The choice of pooling mechanism depends on your individual needs and tax considerations. It is advisable to deal with the topic early on in order to make the shareholder structure more agile and to prevent potential problems in advance of financing rounds or exits. Well-thought-out pooling can help reduce complexity in a growing circle of shareholders and protect investors. Below is a summary of your advantages and disadvantages of the individual solutions.

Type of Solution	Advantages	Disadvantages
Voting Pool	• Most cost-effective alternative quickly implemented	• Angels can still act externally and would only be liable for damages internally • Relatively high administrative effort
Trust Solution	• Angels are no longer on the cap table and therefore have few rights externally	• Trust agreement must be notarized • Costs for trustees are incurred • INVEST grant would have to be repaid if the trust solution is established within the first three years after the angels receive the shares
Pool Company	• Angels are no longer on the cap table and therefore have no rights externally	• INVEST grant would have to be repaid if the trust solution is established within the first three years after the angels receive the shares • Most expensive solution • High administrative effort

g. Financing Round with a VC

Now we want to deal with what you need to consider in a financing round with a professional investor, where caution is required, and what you should personally aim for as a result.

aa) Term Sheet—what is it and what should it contain?

The term sheet is a crucial document in the initial phase of a financing round with a venture capitalist (VC). It is a summary of the main terms of the proposed investment and serves as a framework for the subsequent contract negotiations. While the term sheet is usually not legally binding, it forms an important basis for the creation of the final, binding contracts. It should contain the following key elements:

- **Company valuation and investment amount:** This includes the pre- and post-money valuation of the company and the amount the VC plans to invest.
- **Type of shares:** Determination of whether they are common business shares, preferred shares, or other shares.
- **Dilution protection:** Protective clauses for investors against dilution of their shares in future capital increases.
- **Employee participation plan:** Information on the existing or planned employee participation plan (ESOP).
- **Voting rights and control mechanisms:** Determination of which voting rights the investors receive and whether they have a seat on the board or similar control rights.
- **Milestones and conditions:** Defined business goals that the company must achieve and conditions under which the financing takes place.
- **Information and audit rights:** Rights of investors to receive regular financial and operational information.
- **Representation and warranties:** Assurances of the company about the current status and the accuracy of essential business information.

- **Exclusivity clause:** Obligation of the company not to conduct financing talks with other parties for a certain period.
- **Confidentiality agreement:** Agreement to protect sensitive information exchanged during negotiations.

The term sheet should be clearly and precisely formulated to avoid misunderstandings. It is advisable to seek legal and financial advice when creating and evaluating a term sheet to ensure that the interests of your company and your fellow founders are adequately considered.

bb) VSOP: Who Gives Up Shares?

A major point of contention is regularly from whose shares the pool for the employees is deducted (on this in Staff). Investors usually want this to be assured by the founders. As a founder, however, you have room for negotiation here, which you should also use. Ideally, founders and investors should contribute 50:50 to the pool for employee shares.

cc) Financing Tied to Milestones

Sometimes investors suggest that parts of the financing amount be tied to certain milestones, e.g., once a product has been fully developed or once a certain turnover or a certain number of users has been reached. This approach can only be discouraged, even if you as a founder are sure at the time of negotiation that you will achieve these milestones. If you fail to dissuade the investor from milestones, you should ensure that the milestones are clearly defined when formulating them, so that there is no subsequent dispute about whether the milestones have been met or not.

dd) Liquidation Preferences

Liquidation preferences are a critical element in negotiations with VCs and ensure that investors get their invested capital (and possibly a certain premium) back before the shareholders of the company receive any distribution in the event of a liquidation, sale, or IPO. This serves to protect the investors, especially in scenarios where the company does not reach the expected value. There are various types of liquidation preferences, e.g., "non-participating", where investors either receive their preferred repayment or the corresponding share of the proceeds (but not both), and "participating", where investors receive both the preferred repayment and their share of the remaining proceeds. The exact terms of the liquidation preferences can have a significant impact on the financial return for you and other shareholders in a successful exit and should therefore be carefully negotiated.

ee) Sample Documentation for a Financing Round (GESSI)

GESSI has also developed and provided a complete standard documentation for a financing round. It can be found here: https://standardsinstitute.de/standardvertraege/finanzierungsrunde.

ff) Documents typically required for a VC financing round

1. A participation and shareholder agreement.
2. If necessary, a spousal consent declaration according to § 1365 BGB.
3. A business order for the management.
4. A business order for the advisory board, if its introduction is planned.
5. Certified powers of attorney of the shareholders who do not personally appear at the notary appointment.
6. The notarial record of the extraordinary general meeting in which the resolutions on the amendment or new drafting of the articles of association and capital increase are passed.
7. A (newly drafted) articles of association (partnership agreement).
8. An acceptance declaration for the newly issued business shares.

gg) Due Diligence

As part of the growth and financing strategy of your startup, due diligence plays a central role as it offers potential investors or buyers a deep insight into the business activity and potential of your company.

Preparation and Organization of Due Diligence As a founder of a startup, due diligence is a crucial step in negotiations with investors or potential buyers. Your careful preparation is essential here. Start by organizing all relevant documents in a structured data room. This includes your financial documents, business plans, patents, legal documents, and contracts. A clear structuring of these documents facilitates the process for the auditors and signals professionalism. Make sure to adequately protect confidential information by, for example, only releasing sensitive data in later phases of the audit and protecting the data room with a password.

Legal and Financial Aspects of Due Diligence A core area of due diligence is the legal and financial review of the company. This includes the evaluation of your contracts, license agreements, labor law aspects, and any potential legal disputes. Financial audits include the analysis of previous financing rounds, revenues, expenses, debts, and assets. It is important that you show transparency in these areas and do not withhold any significant information. Undiscovered problems can later lead to negotiation problems, reduce the value of your company, or trigger liability—this must be avoided.

Strategic and Operational Aspects In addition to the legal and financial issues, you should also keep an eye on the strategic and operational aspects of due diligence. This includes the presentation of your business model, your market and competitive analysis, and your corporate strategy. It is important that you clearly communicate your vision and goals and show how your company can achieve them. Also, demonstrating scalability and sustainable growth plays a role. The ability to demonstrate company performance based on KPIs (Key Performance Indicators) can strengthen investor confidence and increase your chances of successful financing.

h. Debt Financing

Debt financing, also known as external financing, is a method of raising capital in which a company borrows money from external sources and commits to repaying the borrowed capital with interest. This differs from the equity financing just discussed, where investors provide capital in exchange for company shares. In debt financing, the company founders retain their ownership shares and do not have to give up control of the company. The repayment of liabilities is made according to a set plan and the interest is often tax-deductible, which offers a financial incentive.

aa) Bank Loans

There are various types of debt financing. Traditional bank loans are the most common form in the SME sector; a fixed amount of money is borrowed and repaid over a certain period with interest. However, bank loans are hardly, if at all, available for start-ups, as they lack extensive assets or stable cash flows, which are required for traditional bank loans.

bb) Venture Debt

Therefore, the category of venture debt has developed. Venture debt is typically provided by specialized lenders or venture debt funds and often complements existing equity financing, for example by venture capital investors.

Unlike traditional loans, which are based on the creditworthiness and assets of a company, venture debt focuses more on the growth potential and previous financing rounds of the company. It is usually short to medium-term and occurs at higher interest rates and often additional compensations such as options on company shares. This reflects the higher risk associated with financing start-ups.

cc) Bonds

Bonds are another option where the company issues debt securities that are purchased by investors. These bonds are traded at a certain interest rate and repayment date.

Each of the methods explained has its own advantages and disadvantages, depending on the needs and financial situation of your company:

- Traditional bank loans:
  - Advantages:

    Fixed interest rates provide predictability in repayments.
    No company share surrender; founders thus retain control.
    Interest is often tax deductible.

  - Disadvantages:

    Often requires collateral and good creditworthiness.
    Fixed repayment plans can be challenging for start-ups with irregular revenues.
    Can be less flexible than other financing methods.

- Venture Debt:
  - Advantages:

    Accessible for start-ups without traditional collateral or stable cash flows.
    Allows growth without immediate further dilution of equity.
    More flexible and often quicker to secure than equity financings.

  - Disadvantages:

    Higher interest rates than traditional loans due to the higher risk.
    Often associated with additional costs such as stock options or warrants.
    Can put pressure on cash flows as regular interest and principal payments are required.

- Bonds:
  - Advantages:

    Allows access to a broader pool of investors.
    Larger sums can often be raised.

  - Disadvantages:

    Can be complex and expensive to issue.
    Fixed interest payments are required regardless of the business situation.

Overall, the choice of financing method strongly depends on the specific needs, the stage of development, and the financial structure of the company. Each option has its own nuances and should be carefully evaluated in the context of the business strategy and objectives.

Staff

a. Staff Recruitment

In our next chapter, we want to dedicate ourselves to the search for the perfect workforce.

The topic of recruitment is a central point in every founding process for building up the company. Because only a qualified, committed, and highly motivated team is capable of turning a profit.

Start-ups particularly encounter difficulties when it comes to competing against established corporations, which often score with their impressive salaries and high degree of security. In such corporations, the workforce can usually be sure that their salary will be in their account at the end of each month. Most start-ups cannot offer such security, especially at the beginning. Their attractiveness lies more in exciting and varied areas of responsibility, which bring a promising dynamic into the company. Precisely because of this apparent deficit, you should focus on a high level of professionalism from the very beginning.

Against this background, the first question arises: What framework conditions should you set for your employee search? Before you deal with your requirements for potential workers, you first need to define

© The Author(s), under exclusive license to Springer Fachmedien Wiesbaden GmbH, part of Springer Nature 2025
B. Quarch et al., *Quick Guide Legal Best Practices for Founders in Germany*, https://doi.org/10.1007/978-3-658-47385-3_4

the conditions you offer. The attractions of a start-up culture with company dynamics despite flat hierarchies are particularly appealing to potential new staff. The conditions consist of the following areas:

1. Remuneration (possibly variable success-based salary component)
2. Possibility of home office
3. Flexitime
4. Vacation days
5. Voluntary social benefits
6. Fringe benefits
7. Development opportunities
8. Participation models

Based on this, you should work out a list that shows your required scope to avoid uncovered personnel costs. You can orientate yourself on the following points for your list:

1. Number of required working hours
2. Work models (full-time, part-time, freelance)
3. Qualifications of the employees

Furthermore, you should be aware that staff recruitment generally requires a high level of resources. The process is not only time-consuming but also requires corresponding financial investments for the job advertisement. Moreover, recruiting involves a certain degree of complexity, which is most efficiently managed through task division. Such a division could be achieved through separate handling of applicant processing, sending feedback, and documenting the key data of potential new employees.

To finally be able to embark on staff recruitment, it is essential for you to identify the best possible platforms for your recruiting. In principle, there is no secret recipe for the "where?" in the search for new employees. Starting with personnel service providers or job portals, through job apps, career networks, social media searches, to job fairs and university recruiting—there are many individual paths that can lead you to your desired result. While working with personnel service providers corresponds more to the traditional way of staff recruitment, especially in highly competitive sectors such as the banking and finance sector in Frankfurt, job portals, which are specialized in industries and job profiles, are the most commonly used form of recruiting today.

Once you have positioned yourself as broadly as possible in terms of reach, the next step is to create a precise requirement profile. Especially at the beginning of every start-up, it is important to keep in mind that tasks can often overlap and clear structures and areas of responsibility will only emerge over time. Nevertheless, from the very beginning, you should always have your clearly defined company goals in mind and consider with each potential new worker how they can contribute to achieving these goals and thus promote the success of the company. This also requires the definition of precise individual skills and abilities that each member of the staff must demonstrate to create a justification for their existence. As a leader, it is up to you to formulate corresponding tasks and requirements related to qualifications.

In doing so, make sure to offer appealing tasks that sound exciting and arouse the interest of the new employee. Here too, your start-up will have many different corners and edges that require numerous individual ideas, which requires creativity. You should therefore set up your team as broadly as possible to cover all areas of responsibility. For these tasks, you should also expect your employees to work independently, characterized by self-motivation, analytics, and communicative skills.

For the evaluation of the necessary professional experience of your future employees, you should at least rely on qualified workers instead of young talents for key positions, who stand out from the start due to their time efficiency and effectiveness. Not to be underestimated in this context is also the component of interpersonal requirements. Every new addition should be able to integrate well into your team and bring an inspiring and ambitious work spirit to promote and challenge the dynamics of the group, rather than working contrarily.

b. Employment Contracts

Once you have assembled the appropriate staff for your company, the next step is to set up employment contracts for them. It is important to note that although a verbal contract is generally also effective and therefore binding for both parties due to freedom of form. However, it is advisable at this point (also because of the so-called "Evidence Act") to formulate the contract in writing and have it signed by both sides to prevent potential future problems.

For questions and problems, innovative consultations for labor law problems such as the company Twinwin (https://www.twin.win/) are available to you.

An employment contract regulates the duties and rights of the workforce and includes the designation as well as the start and duration of the employment relationship, the main area of activity, information on working hours, remuneration, vacation, secondary activities, non-competition clause, termination as well as the notice period and a confidentiality agreement.

Content of the employment contract

- Preamble
- Start and term
- Focus of activity
- Working hours
- Remuneration
- Vacation
- Secondary employment and non-competition clause
- Termination
- Confidentiality agreement

aa) Designation

The designation of the contract can vary and is composed of the following pool:

- (un)limited or project-related employment contract
- Employment contract for part-time employees or temporary workers
- Employment contract for freelancers
- Employment contract for mini-jobs
- Employment contract for interns

The legal basis for each individual contract is the Basic Law, the Civil Code, the collective agreement as well as company and individual agreements.

bb) Start and Duration

After you have clarified the start of the employment relationship with your newly acquired employees, you should consider whether you want to conclude a fixed-term or permanent contract with them. Depending on the term, it must be written down until when the employment relationship should exist. Make sure that a fixed-term contract without a factual reason is not effective beyond two years and you are then obliged to either make the employee permanent or end the employment relationship. It is also important that you are allowed to extend a potentially fixed-term contract a maximum of three times within this period.

In addition to agreements on the start and duration of the employment relationship, it may be useful for you as an employer to set a three- to six-month probationary period for your staff. Such a period serves to test the suitability of your future employees. During the probationary period, you are entitled to give notice without a reason for termination within 14 days. Please note that if a new employment contract has been agreed with already employed workers, the option of a probationary period is denied to you.

cc) Main Area of Activity

The main area of activity describes all the tasks and duties expected from your employees in the future. Try not to choose too precise formulations if possible, in order to cover as broad a range of activities as possible.

dd) Working Hours

When it comes to working hours, it is first necessary to formulate the weekly hourly working time as well as the start and end times. It is important that your staff, as a rule, should not exceed a working time of eight hours per working day. In addition, after a maximum of six hours of activity, a break of at least 30 minutes must be taken, provided that the daily working time is up to nine hours. Otherwise, the break must be at least 45 minutes, with a division of the time span of at least 15 minutes per block being possible.

Furthermore, you have the option to offer flexible working hours, i.e., the free choice of working hours by your workforce within a fixed framework, instead of fixed times.

ee) Remuneration

The sub-point of remuneration describes the monthly gross salary of your employee as well as the due date of the payment. The salary can consist not only of the basic salary, but also of possible bonuses, special payments or profit distributions through possible employee participations.

Special caution is required with the clause that overtime is covered by the salary. This is always legally ineffective. Also rigid exclusion periods, after which remuneration or all claims expire if they are not asserted in time, are problematic. There are one-stage (assertion of a claim within a period) and two-stage (filing a lawsuit regarding the claim within another period after the assertion) exclusion periods. An exclusion period of less than 3 months is invalid, as is the exclusion of claims to the minimum wage. Nothing stricter may be agreed than the assertion of a claim in text form (§ 309 No. 23a BGB). If the second stage has been inappropriately designed, only this is omitted. If the first stage is already invalid, the second one also falls away (blue pencil test).

ff) Vacation

As an employer, you are obliged to grant your staff a minimum annual vacation. Depending on the number of working days per week, this is 20 days for a 5-day week and 24 days for a 6-day week. In addition, you must consider whether your employees are obliged to take the vacation within the calendar year or whether you allow them to carry it over to the following year.

In addition, there is the possibility to record in writing a waiting period for taking the vacation. By law, there is a waiting period of six months from the start of the activity (§ 4 BUrlG).

gg) Secondary Activities and Non-Competition Clause

The employment contract should also contain precise provisions on secondary activities and any non-competition clauses. Secondary activities include any activity of the workforce that is carried out outside of work, such as employment relationships with another company, unpaid and voluntary activities or self-employed secondary activities. If this could affect the work obligation of your staff, they should be obliged to report it. Under certain circumstances, it may be useful to prevent future employees from doing further business in your line of business and thus establishing a competitive relationship as part of the non-competition clause.

hh) Confidentiality Agreement

The last point on our checklist is the confidentiality agreement. This states that your staff must treat information concerning your company, for example regarding business and trade secrets, data protection, telecommunications secrecy and social secrecy, confidentially. The legal consequence of a breach of the confidentiality agreement is the criminal liability of the abusing employees.

c. Central Labor Law Provisions

As a founder, you are not only an entrepreneur, but also an employer for your employees. Therefore, you should familiarize yourself with some basic provisions of labor law that apply to you when initiating the employment relationship, during its execution, and during and after its termination.

aa) Initiation and Establishment of the Employment Relationship

To find suitable employees, you should make your recruiting attractive as described and point out the advantages of a position with you. Applicants are generally not obliged to disclose any information or details about themselves. This only applies if the applicants are obviously unsuitable for the position under all aspects or if certain characteristics are particularly decisive for the performance of the work.

Subsequently, you must ask the applicants appropriate questions to find out if candidates are suitable for the position. However, caution is required when developing a list of questions: Some questions in the job interview are not permissible. It is always a question of the individual case when there is still a legitimate interest in information or when the question infringes too much on the personal rights of future employees. It is permissible to ask about qualifications or professional career, but a question about pregnancy, disability or diseases, as well as party membership, for example, is not permissible. Applicants do not have to answer impermissible questions truthfully, they are expressly allowed to lie in this respect.

If applicants give an incorrect answer to a permissible question or violate their disclosure obligations, this can be classified as fraudulent deception, which entitles to contestation according to § 123 para. 1 Alt. 1 BGB. In this way, you can subsequently cancel the employment relationship if you learn of a lie from the job interview. If there is a justified lie as a result of an impermissible question, there is no unlawful deception and therefore no right to contest. Normally, a contestation has retroactive effect, i.e., the employment relationship would be considered null and void from the beginning. However, this would mean that the parties would have to mutually return everything they have obtained during the previous execution of the employment relationship. This is not so easy due to the permanent exchange of services. Therefore, in labor law, a contestation is not assumed to have retroactive invalidity as usual. The employment relationship is considered lawful for the past due to the mutual exchange of services, and only for the future does the employer have a right to repudiate (doctrine of the factual employment relationship). This only applies if no exchange of services has yet taken place, the contestation has its usual retroactive effect. These principles also apply to all other reasons that can lead to the nullity of the employment relationship. For example, if the employee is incapable of contracting (§ 104, 105 BGB) or the employment contract is immoral (§ 138 para. 1 BGB).

bb) Obligations and Rights Arising from the Employment Relationship

On the one hand, employees are primarily obliged to perform the agreed work. As already described, the work obligation should not be agreed too narrowly. Employers have a right of direction from § 106 GewO and can thus broadly deploy employees within the scope of the roughly agreed activity. Since the employment contract is a service contract according to § 611a BGB, employees do not owe a specific success, but the activity itself. Therefore, employers can only demand the quality of work that employees can perform with reasonable effort without endangering their health. An objective minimum performance can be expected, but not a specific result of the work performance. In addition to this main obligation, employees have a secondary obligation to refrain from anything that contradicts the interests of the employers. For example, they must not thwart the achievement of the contractual goal, damage the employer's property, behave disloyally, and not disclose business secrets. They are also obliged to surrender what they have obtained from the execution of the work (§ 667 Alt. 2 BGB).

On the other hand, employers are primarily obliged to remunerate the work. The amount of the remuneration is primarily determined by the employment contract. The remuneration must not be below the minimum wage (§ 1 para. 1, 2, § 3 MiLoG). However, a claim to special payments can also result from a company practice, i.e., repeated voluntary services on the part of the employers. After a certain time, employees acquire a legal claim that this service will continue to be granted. Therefore, such a payment should always be made with the express reference to its uniqueness, even if the special payment is to be granted again next year. As secondary obligations, employers have to avoid dangers for their employees, protect their personal and other rights at the workplace and above all treat all employees equally in the sense of the AGG. An unjustifiable unequal treatment of employees can result in a liability for damages or compensation according to § 15 para. 1, 2 AGG.

The obligation to pay remuneration is fundamentally waived if the employees do not fulfill their work obligations (§ 326 para. 1 sentence 1 BGB). However, there are numerous exceptions in favor of your employees, so you are still obliged to pay wages: You are responsible for the fact that the employees cannot work (§ 326 para. 2 sentence 1 BGB), you cannot or do not want to accept the service (§ 615 BGB), the employees are prevented for a short period for personal reasons (§ 616 sentence 1 BGB), they are absent due to illness without fault for up to six weeks (§ 3 para. 1 sentence 1 EFZG), they take vacation leave (§ 1 BUrlG) or there are holidays (§ 2 para. 2 EFZG). If employees do not perform the work as desired, a reduction in wages is not provided for. A claim for damages only comes into consideration if you suffer an actual loss of integrity beyond mere poor performance. Note that you must demonstrate the breach of duty by your employees according to § 619a BGB. Other breaches of duty in addition to poor work performance can also lead to an employee's liability under § 280 para. 1 BGB, possibly in conjunction with § 241 para. 2 BGB, or § 823 para. 1 BGB. However, in the case of company-induced activity, employees are always limited in their liability and a distribution between the parties takes place according to the degree of fault (so-called internal damage compensation): For intent and gross negligence, the employees alone are liable, for slight negligence employees are not liable and in the case of medium negligence, the liability is apportioned on a case-by-case basis.

Your employees have a claim against you for reimbursement of their expenses, which they incurred and reasonably could have incurred in the course of their work (§ 670 BGB analogously). This claim can even extend to typical accompanying damages associated with the activity, which employees suffer themselves (§ 670 BGB doubly analogously). If the employer does not fully comply with his contractual obligations, he may be liable under § 280 para. 1, possibly in conjunction with § 241 para. 2 BGB or § 823 para. 1 BGB. In particular, a violation of the general right of personality or discrimination in the workplace may be considered. An unjustifiable unequal treatment of employees can result in a liability for damages or compensation under § 15 para. 1, 2 AGG. If the remuneration is not paid (on time) by you, a liability under § 286 BGB is threatened.

cc) Termination of Employment

Employment can end in many different ways: the expiration of an agreed term, termination by mutual agreement, contestation or renunciation, or—as in most cases—dismissal.

There is a distinction between extraordinary and ordinary dismissal.

In the case of ordinary dismissal, the employment relationship is terminated at the end of a notice period. This period ranges from one to seven months depending on the length of service (§ 622 para. 1, 2

BGB). The dismissal may not be without reason from the employer's side if the conditions of the Dismissal Protection Act apply. The KSchG applies according to § 23 KSchG usually only if you have more than 10 employees.

Under these circumstances, the dismissal must be justified by a reason, whether it is a personal dismissal (the reason for dismissal is based on the person of the employee), behavioral dismissal (the reason for dismissal is based on changeable behaviors of the employee), or operational dismissal (the reason for dismissal is an urgent operational requirement that makes continued employment impossible). In each case, you must proceed in the same way when determining whether a dismissal of specific employees is lawful:

1. **Reason for dismissal itself:** Is there an abstract (personal, behavioral, operational) reason why I want to end the relationship?
2. **Forecast:** Is it to be assumed based on a forecast that the characteristics, behaviors, or circumstances leading to dismissal will continue in the future?
3. **Ultima Ratio:** Are there milder means than dismissal (such as a warning or assignment to another workplace)?
4. **Balancing:** Does my interest in termination outweigh the interests of the employees in continued employment (for example, the extent of disruption and impairment, duration of misconduct, alternative employment opportunities, age)?
5. **In the case of personal dismissal:** Are my operational interests significantly impaired by continued employment?
6. **In the case of operational dismissal:** Does the dismissal withstand the social selection according to § 1 para. 3 KSchG, i.e., do I dismiss from a group of comparable employees according to the weighting of the social criteria from § 1 para. 3 sentence 1 KSchG and non-inclusion of employees according to § 1 para. 3 sentence 2 KSchG the least deserving person?

The ordinary dismissal must be declared in writing (§ 623 BGB) and can be pronounced on the fifteenth or at the end of a calendar month.

In the case of extraordinary dismissal, the employment relationship is terminated immediately without any further notice period. Since it particularly burdens the employees, an important reason according to § 626 para. 1 BGB is necessary, which justifies the immediate termination. It can be done informally, but must be declared within two weeks after becoming aware of the reason justifying dismissal. The same reasons as for an ordinary dismissal can be considered, but it must be considered whether a milder means, such as an ordinary dismissal, is possible and it must be carefully weighed whether the behavior justifies termination without any further notice period. If the extraordinary dismissal is based on the suspicion of criminal behavior, the dismissal is not due to the crime, but due to the shattered trust relationship. However, this is only permissible if there is a certain probability of actual commission, the employees were heard about the incident, and you have taken all reasonable steps to resolve the incident and dispel the suspicion.

d. ESOP Employee Participation

Employee Stock Ownership Plans (ESOP) are a popular means of involving employees in the company by granting them shares or stock options. This form of employee participation serves not only as an incentive and reward, but also promotes their attachment to the company and motivates higher performance, as they are directly involved in the success of the company. With the new Growth Opportunities Act, which aims to promote start-ups and growth-oriented companies, innovations have been introduced in the area of employee participation. These changes make it easier for companies to offer ESOPs by removing tax and legal obstacles. For example, the tax regulations have been adjusted so that the taxation of benefits from stock options only occurs upon the sale of the shares, instead of already at the exercise of the options. This reduces the liquidity burden for employees. These innovations make ESOPs more attractive and accessible for start-ups and contribute to attracting and retaining qualified talent, which is crucial for the growth and success of these companies.

Rules of Procedure for the Management

In our next chapter, we will discuss the topic of rules of procedure for the management. Normally, the articles of association contain a clause that allows the shareholders' meeting to issue rules of procedure and, if necessary, to amend them with the necessary majority. The rules of procedure are a link between the articles of association—which can only be amended by notarial act—and the managing director's service contract, which usually also refers to the rules of procedure.

There is generally no obligation to create rules of procedure for the management and to adopt them in the company. The essential scope of action for the managing directors is already formulated in the management contract, the articles of association, and in any case in the law. However, if your start-up's management is staffed by several people, the operation of the business usually requires the managing directors to coordinate all organizational matters among themselves, for which a binding set of rules, or an internal set of rules related to the working method, is needed. This can narrowly define the scope of action for the management and ensure information obligations towards the shareholders. An installed distribution of tasks (the so-called departmental

© The Author(s), under exclusive license to Springer Fachmedien Wiesbaden GmbH, part of Springer Nature 2025

B. Quarch et al., *Quick Guide Legal Best Practices for Founders in Germany*,
https://doi.org/10.1007/978-3-658-47385-3_5

distribution) does not change the fact that the managing directors must monitor and inform each other.

In principle, you can determine a chair of the management. This person then has the particular task of coordinating business areas, leading meetings, representing the shareholders' meeting, and taking on a representative role.

a. Process Flow—Communication, Decision and Filing

The rules of procedure you have adopted should cover various aspects of the process flow regarding communication, decision-making, and filing. They should define businesses in which the management may only act with the approval of the shareholders' meeting.

Important regulations about communication include the determination of communication tools and channels. This can be done, for example, through email traffic, phone calls, or regular meetings. Also relevant are provisions on responsibilities for internal and external communication, general rules regarding communication with shareholders, customers, business contacts, and staff, as well as the determination for the handling of various concerns.

Regarding decision-making, you should include provisions on responsibilities and decision-making powers of the management. Furthermore, it is necessary to find regulations for the recording of decisions and the procedure for decision-making (unanimity principle or majority decisions) as well as the participation and voting rights at meetings of all shareholders.

In the area of filing, it is up to you to make various decisions. This includes the determination of regulations for data protection and access rights, the determination of document filing and archiving, and the handling of sensitive data and confidential information. In this context, you should also decide how the storage of documents should be carried out.

In addition, there are some other provisions that you can also include in the rules of procedure. These include guidelines for planning and conducting meetings, the determination of regular reporting obligations, regulations on the delegation of tasks, and responsibilities within the company structure. Furthermore, the rules of procedure can have effects on the liability of individual managing directors in case of possible wrong decisions through the business distribution plan. For investors, clauses regarding reporting obligations, such as the intervals and contents of the information obligations of the management towards the members, are also relevant. Last but not least, the rules of procedure can regulate details (timing and content) of the company planning for the upcoming year or even multi-year planning.

b. Typical Transactions Requiring Approval

A crucial element of the rules of procedure are the so-called transactions requiring approval, which are intended to set limits on the management by obliging them to ask the shareholders' meeting for approval for certain projects. This project must then be approved by a majority previously defined in the rules of procedure. If managers violate the approval requirement, they can be accused of a breach of duty, which in serious cases can even lead to dismissal. It is advisable not to set too narrow limits, as otherwise necessary decisions can be delayed by strict restrictions in the rules of procedure.

The rules of procedure also establish a catalogue of transactions requiring approval. A distinction is made between typical and atypical transactions requiring approval. Typical transactions requiring approval describe transactions where the approval requirement generally arises from legal provisions, their requirements are therefore legally regulated and clearly defined. The following are typical transactions requiring approval to be listed in the rules of procedure:

1. Change of the company's object or areas of activity
2. Adoption of business plans (investment planning, profit and loss account or other budget planning)
3. Capital measures: Increase of the share capital, issue of new business shares or the withdrawal of business shares

4. Taking out loans or credits from a certain order of magnitude
5. Disposal of assets (e.g. real estate or subsidiaries)
6. Waiver of claims or legal disputes from a specific, usually mentioned in the rules of procedure, amount
7. Mergers and acquisitions
8. Conclusion of long-term contracts (e.g. lease agreements, lease agreements, cooperation agreements or supply contracts)
   → Here, only measures that would result in deviations from the previously mentioned plans are usually relevant. The rules of procedure usually describe a buffer to leave enough room for the management in day-to-day business.
9. Dissolution or liquidation of the company
10. Granting or revocation of power of attorney given to employees
11. Detailed tasks and responsibilities of the advisory board, if one exists

Always keep in mind that the points mentioned above are not exhaustive. Depending on the form of the company and individual agreement, further transactions requiring approval may be added.

c. Atypical Transactions Requiring Approval

In contrast to typical transactions requiring approval, atypical transactions requiring approval include those transactions that are not explicitly regulated by law and therefore result from individual party agreements. In particular, this refers to special contract clauses that require approval for explicit actions or transactions. Atypical transactions requiring approval thus represent more specific cases that arise in the course of extraordinary circumstances or individual agreements. The following are atypical transactions requiring approval to be listed in the rules of procedure:

1. Sale or transfer of business shares
2. Change of the company structure (e.g. the transformation of the company from a GmbH into an AG)

3. Extraordinary business incidents (e.g. the taking up of extraordinary loans, the assumption of significant liabilities or extraordinary purchases, such as those of cryptocurrencies)

d. Sample of Rules of Procedure

Fundamentally, it is important for you to understand that your business rules should be individually tailored to your company and its specific requirements. Therefore, it is recommended at this point to involve all groups of people in the creation of the business rules. An example can be found at https://www.soldan.de/media/pdf/c6/65/a4/9783955542887_LP.pdf:

> "The shareholders' meeting of the …….. GmbH has decided on the following rules of procedure for the management of the company in accordance with § 5 para. 4 of the articles of association:
>
> **§ 1 Rules of Procedure**
>
> 1. The management consists of at least two managing directors. The members of the management are appointed and dismissed by the shareholders' meeting.
> 2. The members of the management conduct the business in accordance with the laws, the articles of association, these rules of procedure, and the instructions of the shareholders' meeting.
>
> **§ 2 Distribution of Business/Chairmanship**
>
> The shareholders' meeting can assign specific tasks and business areas to each managing director. The details are determined by a business distribution plan to be decided by it.
>
> **§ 3 Distribution of Business/Chairmanship**
>
> 1. The shareholders' meeting can assign specific tasks and business areas to each managing director. The details are determined by a business distribution plan to be decided by it.
> 2. If more than two managing directors are appointed, the shareholders' meeting is to determine a chairman of the management. This person

is responsible for coordinating the management. The managing directors have to report to the chairman of the management and are bound by his instructions, as long as the instruction is in accordance with the law and the articles of association.
3. Furthermore, in the case of paragraph 2, the shareholders' meeting determines a deputy chairman who steps into the tasks and powers of the chairman in case of his absence.

§ 4 Duties of the Managing Directors

1. Each managing director conducts the business or the tasks and/or the business area assigned to him independently and on his own responsibility.
2. Measures and transactions that are or can be of particular importance for the legal or economic situation of the company or the company's position in public must be reported immediately to the chairman of the management. If a chairman is not determined, the notification must be made to the other managing director(s).
3. The managing directors require the prior approval by resolution of the shareholders for all transactions and measures, as was decided by the shareholders' meeting in a catalog of transactions requiring approval in accordance with § 5 para. 5 of the articles of association.
4. In cases of extreme urgency, the managing directors are entitled to act without the prior approval of the shareholders' meeting if they may assume under the circumstances that the latter would approve the deviation if they were aware of the situation (emergency measure). If a chairman of the management is determined, his approval is necessary for the implementation of the emergency measure. The shareholders' meeting must be informed immediately with a request for approval.

§ 5 Management Meetings

1. The managing directors should meet regularly, at least every two weeks, for management meetings. Each managing director is entitled to convene management meetings.
2. All matters of fundamental and essential importance for the company are to be discussed in the management meetings. The results of the management meetings are recorded in minutes, which are to be sent

to the members of the management and the recipient authorized by the shareholders' meeting.

3. Each managing director is entitled to make proposals for the agenda.
Place, date, signatures of the minute taker or the shareholders"

e. Approval Reservations for Management

aa) Statutory Provision in a GmbH

It is sensible to anchor the possibility of restricting the management authority of the managing directors in the articles of association. This is because changing the articles of association requires a qualified majority of three quarters of the votes cast by the shareholders and must also be notarized (§ 53 para. 2 GmbHG). The more control rights are anchored in the articles of association, the easier it is to transfer the majority of the company shares to the acquiring party in the course of a business succession. It is then sufficient for the transferring party to retain only the blocking minority in the company. Such a statutory provision provides a flexible basis for coordinating and adjusting the interests of the management and the participants.

In accordance with paragraph 4 of the following model provision, the manner of management is regulated by the shareholders. In accordance with paragraph 5 of the following model provision, the type and scope of transactions requiring approval can be regulated, changed and supplemented by shareholder resolution. The statutory provision can have the following wording:

"**§ 5 Management and Representation**

1. The company has one or more managing directors. If only one managing director is appointed, then he represents the company alone.
2. If several managing directors are appointed, then two managing directors are jointly authorized to represent the company. If there are authorized signatories and several managing directors, a managing director is also authorized to represent the company in conjunction with an authorized signatory.

3. The shareholders can grant a managing director individual power of representation by shareholder resolution and exempt the managing director from the restrictions of § 181 BGB.
4. The managing directors are obliged to conduct the company's business in accordance with the law, this partnership agreement and the resolutions of the shareholders.
5. The managing directors require the prior approval by shareholder resolution for all transactions which the shareholders declare to be subject to approval by shareholder resolution."

bb) Catalog of Transactions Requiring Approval

Based on this statutory provision, a catalog of transactions requiring approval can be adopted. The following model for a catalog of transactions requiring approval is intended as a checklist. Such a catalog must be adapted to the individual case. With regard to the need for approval, it should be noted that the procedure should be practicable. It should be avoided that the approval of often short-term transactions fails because a shareholders' meeting cannot be held in time. If the catalog of transactions requiring approval is rather extensive, it is advisable for the participants to set up a separate committee of shareholders who take over this competence for all participants. This can also be an advisory board that simultaneously provides advisory services to the managing directors.

Investor Relations

Let's now focus on how to operationally deal with one's investors, or rather, how one must deal with them. If these have become shareholders in the company in the sense of the GmbH Act through capital increase or conversion, they already have extensive rights, so-called shareholder rights, by law. These rights can vary depending on the specific regulations in the articles of association of the GmbH.

a. Shareholder Rights According to the GmbH Act

It is important that founders familiarize themselves with the legal framework to understand what rights investors have. The following are the most important shareholder rights that founders need to know and implement:

© The Author(s), under exclusive license to Springer Fachmedien Wiesbaden GmbH, part of Springer Nature 2025

B. Quarch et al., *Quick Guide Legal Best Practices for Founders in Germany*, https://doi.org/10.1007/978-3-658-47385-3_6

1. **Voting rights (§ 47 GmbHG)**: Shareholders generally have a voting right in the shareholders' meeting and in a shareholders' resolution, unless the law or the articles of association provide otherwise. Voting rights are usually distributed according to the amount of the respective shareholder's business share.
2. **Participation in meetings:** Participants have the right to attend shareholders' meetings. The shareholders' meeting is generally convened by the management (§ 49 GmbHG). Shareholders whose business shares cumulatively or alone correspond to at least 10% of the company's share capital are entitled to request the convening of the shareholders' meeting (§ 50 GmbHG).
3. **Right to information (§ 51a GmbHG)**: Shareholders have the right to inform themselves about the affairs of the GmbH. This includes the right to inspect the business documents, as far as this is necessary for the exercise of shareholder rights. They can request information about the affairs of the GmbH from the management. However, this right may be limited if there is a predominant interest of the company or other shareholders against it.
4. **Claim to profits (§ 29 GmbHG):** Participants are entitled to a share of the annual surplus plus carryforward of the GmbH, which is usually proportional to their business shares. However, the exact distribution can be determined in the articles of association.
5. **Liquidation share (§ 72 GmbHG):** In the event of the dissolution of the GmbH, shareholders are entitled to a share of the liquidation proceeds after all liabilities have been settled. Here too, the distribution is usually based on the business shares.

Shareholders therefore actually have many rights and can significantly reduce the leeway of the founders. It is therefore worthwhile to pool as many shareholders as possible (see Financing) in order to bind voting rights and limit powers. In particular, the co-determination rights mean that, for example, in a financing round with new investors, approval must be obtained. If shareholders oppose, they can block the entire financing round in the worst case.

b. In Practice: Monthly Reportings

Now, founders rightly ask themselves how these rights are actually exercised in practice. Typically, start-up founders send a report via email to the investors at the end of the month, often referred to as „Investor Update" or „Monthly Reporting". What exactly this reporting should contain is partly stipulated in the SHA („Shareholders Agreement") and should be discussed practically again after the financing round. How much detail is included in these reports is up to the founders. However, at least the current figures should be communicated, i.e., how much revenue was gained/lost in the last month, what is the total revenue, how much money was spent („Burn"), current account balances, and how long the money will last („Runway"). Often there are also special Excel templates provided by the investors, into which this information must also be entered. It is also common to report on relevant developments such as team composition, new hires, and commercial successes.

Example Structure of a Report

1. Highlights of the last month
2. Lowlights of the last month
3. Figures
4. Sales & Marketing
5. Product Developments
6. HR
7. Outlook: Goals for the next month
8. Asks (How investors can specifically help)

In addition to the written reporting, a cycle is often agreed upon in shareholder agreements in which meetings must take place. These are often also scheduled monthly.

c. Board Management

From a certain size, usually in the seed round or Series A, a board is also legally agreed upon, to which certain shareholder rights (see above) can be transferred, for example, certain transactions. Typical transactions that require the approval of the board include, for example, the hiring of new employees who are to receive a salary above €100,000 or general expenditures that exceed a certain amount. It is also agreed upon how often the board should meet.

It is worth treating board meetings professionally from the start and preparing and following up well. The following best practices apply even more so to shareholder meetings if no advisory board/board has been set up.

1. **Agenda:** In any case, founders should ideally send an agenda along with the invitation so that all board members know what topics will be discussed.
2. **Presentation and Documents:** It is also best practice to circulate the relevant meeting documents to be discussed in advance, especially contracts or financial documents.
3. **Moderation of the Meeting:** It is up to the founders to lead the meeting efficiently. This means working through the agenda and at the same time addressing points that are raised outside the agenda without the meeting being „hijacked". If board members tend to drift into long discussions, it is advisable to timebox the agenda items so that everyone knows, for example, that 10 minutes of discussion are planned for the next item and then the decision-making follows.
4. **Documentation:** The board meetings should always be well documented. In particular, this refers to decisions and individual votes of the respective board members. The minutes should be made available to all participants afterwards.

Good Governance for Managing Directors

Let's now deal with the legal foundations, obligations, and best practices that all managing directors of a UG (limited liability) or GmbH should know and comply with.

a. Convening Ordinary/Extraordinary Shareholders' Meeting

As a managing director, you are obliged to convene the shareholders' meeting when it appears necessary in the interest of the company. You have a certain amount of discretion in this regard. When in doubt, you should always consider convening a shareholders' meeting when an extraordinary situation arises, i.e., whenever the assets of the GmbH are threatened, when extraordinary transactions are concluded, or when it comes to transactions that are not within the scope of the GmbH. An example of this is the purchase of a property by the GmbH.

Regardless of such events, you have to convene the so-called ordinary shareholders' meeting once a year as a managing director to decide on

© The Author(s), under exclusive license to Springer Fachmedien Wiesbaden GmbH, part of Springer Nature 2025
B. Quarch et al., *Quick Guide Legal Best Practices for Founders in Germany*, https://doi.org/10.1007/978-3-658-47385-3_7

matters that are subject to the provisions of the shareholders, among other things.

b. Obligation to Deposit Balance Sheet and Accounting

Once a year, as a managing director, you have the obligation to prepare a balance sheet, to decide on the determination of the annual financial statements or the balance sheet and on the use of the results, and finally to deposit the balance sheet with the Federal Gazette.

In the first fiscal year after your foundation, you initially have no to-dos here, but this does not exempt you from the obligation to keep the books of the GmbH correctly even in this year. It makes sense to bring a tax consultant on board for this. When choosing a tax consultant, it is advisable to look for someone with start-up experience.

c. Preparation of Tax Returns

As the tax responsible person of the GmbH, you must ensure that the tax returns (corporate tax, trade tax, and sales tax return) are submitted by May 31 of the year following the fiscal year at the latest. If the tax consultant prepares the tax returns, the submission deadline is extended to September 30 of the following year. At the request of the tax consultant, this deadline can be extended to December 31 of the following year or even further in justified exceptional cases (e.g., illness).

d. Tax Registrations

As a managing director, you are obliged to submit tax registrations for the GmbH. This includes the advance VAT return, the wage tax registration, and the capital gains tax registration.

The tax registrations must be submitted to the tax office no later than 10 days (i.e., by the 10th of the following month) after the end of the registration period.

Newly established companies must submit advance notifications monthly for the first two years. Upon request, an extension of one month can be granted. Tax registrations and pre-registrations are carried out electronically (www.businessregister.de).

However, you should not take this on yourself, but instead hire a tax consultant for the tax registrations. These tax registrations are the daily bread of tax consultants and the costs for this are manageable.

e. Obligation to Maintain Share Capital

As a managing director, you are responsible for ensuring that the assets, which are responsible for maintaining the share capital, are not paid out to the shareholders. Payouts are only permissible if the net assets of the company (= sum of the assets; borrowed capital + provisions) are greater than the stated share capital figure. This results from the commercial balance sheet of your company. In the case of a GmbH, the share capital is usually EUR 25000. If violated, a repayment obligation of the shareholders arises. As a shareholder or managing director, you would be personally liable. You would then have to reimburse the amounts paid out to the GmbH from your own assets.

Against this background, you should regularly check your net assets.

f. Obligation to File for Insolvency and Prohibition of Payments

Things don't always go smoothly: Unfortunately, it can happen that things don't go as you planned and you slowly run out of money. In a crisis, the duties of the managing director change. The most important duties in a crisis, which you should have heard of, are summarized below:

aa) Obligation to File for Insolvency

If one of the two reasons for insolvency (inability to pay and over-indebtedness) occurs, you must generally file for insolvency immediately or, if there are prospects for restructuring, within three weeks in the event of insolvency or six weeks in the event of over-indebtedness. If you do not do this, you can even be prosecuted.

bb) Prohibition of Payments

WARNING Regardless of the obligation to file for insolvency, you face severe personal liability if you do not also immediately stop your company's payment transactions when insolvency occurs. For each prohibited payment you make for the company, you are liable with your personal assets. From the onset of insolvency, you may only make payments that are „compatible with the care of a prudent and conscientious business manager". What is meant by this is not clearly defined either in law or by case law. Therefore, to be on the safe side, you should only make payments from the onset of insolvency that are expressly permitted.
The following payments are expressly permitted:

- Payment of the employee's share of the social security contribution
- Payments which, if not made, would lead to the immediate cessation of business operations, e.g.
  - Electricity
  - Water
  - Heating
  - (partially) wages and salaries
  - Rent of business premises
  - a reasonable remuneration for the restructuring advisor

Also, in a crisis and before the onset of insolvency, you must be careful not to make any payment to the shareholders of your company that leads to insolvency. Because here too, you are personally liable for such prohibited payments.

Because of the risk of liability associated with this, it is recommended to regularly check for the possible occurrence of reasons for insolvency.

g. Legal Basis for Personal Liability

i. Managing directors can be personally liable

In particular, GmbH managing directors often believe that they are protected by the mandatory contribution of 25,000 € and do not have to fear any further liability. We also often hear that business leaders assume that there is only a risk of personal liability if they intentionally violate a legal obligation. However, many high-profile trials in recent years have shown that business leaders who violate their duties of care are exposed to significant claims—even in the case of simple negligence.

Failure to comply with the required care can result in personal liability to the company: For this very reason, Deutsche Bank demanded damages of 3.5 billion € from its former CEO, Rolf Breuer, as a result of the sensational Leo Kirch affair*e*.

Whether and how much a manager is liable depends on the so-called standard of care:

Managing directors (GmbH) must apply the „care of a prudent (and conscientious) business manager“ in conducting business (according to § 43 I GmbHG).

This standard applies to all actions of business leaders, especially in terms of supervisory duties and decisions.

If these decisions are not made based on the standard of care or if it cannot be proven in a dispute that this was adhered to, the business leaders are **personally** liable.

1. Consequences of Breach of Duty If business leaders have breached a duty, this can result in a significant claim for damages or clawback. The reliability of the business leaders can also be questioned, which in turn can deny their suitability to lead a company. The breach of a duty can also have employment law consequences: business leaders can be dismissed.

You should be aware of these possible consequences of breach of duty:

a. Damages (§ 43 II GmbHG) the company can demand from business leaders who violate their duty of care or who cannot prove that they have fulfilled their duty of care.

- **The claim amount is unlimited** and can cover all losses of the company—which can easily lead to the **personal bankruptcy of the business leaders**.
- Business leaders are **required to provide proof („burden of proof reversal")** and must therefore prove that they have fulfilled their duty of care—often many years later.

b. Clawback (§§ 18, 20 InstitutsVergVO, § 87 AktG) means the right to reclaim the entire variable remuneration (i.e., bonuses) of the business leader of the last (at least) 5 years in case of violation of behavioral and decency norms or if the behavior of the business leader has led to significant losses or a regulatory intervention. However, this claim will usually not be relevant for start-up CEOs, as variable remuneration is usually not paid.

WARNING Long limitation periods: Even if business leaders have already left, these claims can be made against them. In the case of a breach of duty, the limitation period is at least 5 years after the damage has occurred, with the affected parties having to prove their innocence. For listed companies, the liability even lasts 10 years.

ii. Understanding Internal and External Liability

If business leaders are personally liable, they are generally liable to the company (according to a claim for damages under § 43 II GmbHG and the clawback claims). However, external third parties can also hold the management accountable in some cases.

1. Internal Liability If business leaders are liable to the **company**, the principle is: The business leaders **must** be held accountable by the company in such a case—this is not a discretionary decision, but a binding decision of the company's bodies and representatives. This means, **the company is generally obliged to sue the business leaders.**

In the case of a GmbH, it is usually the **shareholders' meeting** itself that asserts claims against the managing directors. If the GmbH has an **advisory board**, this duty can often be transferred to it.

2. Claims also threatened by external third parties Liability for breach of duty towards third parties can also lead to claims by outsiders against the management personally. The following institutions, for example, can assert claims directly against the members of the management, for example under *§ 69 AO* (taxes) or *§ 826 BGB* (intentional immoral damage):

- Social insurance carriers
- Tax office, e.g., investigations and proceedings in tax matters
- Insolvency administrators
- Data protection authorities
- Banks
- Customers, suppliers, and competitors

iii. Legal Protection Against Personal Liability

To protect yourself from these consequences, you should definitely take preventive measures and secure yourself as a business manager. The following three precautions are recommended for the best possible protection against liability cases:

1. **Exemption measures prevent personal liability**: The exemption measures that make sense depend on whether it is a bound or a business decision (see iv. in detail).
2. **Documentation proves the implementation of exemption measures**: The decision-making process must be thoroughly **documented**. The documentation of the decision-making process should then be systematically **filed** and stored.
3. **Insurances protect when a liability case has occurred.** These insurances are considered:

- D&O insurances
- Criminal legal protection insurances
- Employment contract legal protection
- Financial loss legal protection

iv. Type of Decisions
Which exemption measures are effective depends on the **type of decision**. Therefore, the first step is to identify whether it is a **legally bound** or **business decision** for business managers. Depending on this, completely different criteria apply as to how to proceed for exemption and how the respective decision is to be evaluated afterwards when checking any liability claims.

1. **Business Decisions** A business decision is made when there is a choice between several lawful options based on assumptions, forecasts, and the exercise of discretion.

Examples: Evaluation, deal structure, purchase of a company, hiring a leadership role, etc.

Business managers must reasonably assume that they have sufficient information and make a decision for the benefit of the company when making a business decision. It should be noted that business managers are not liable for economic failures—they are not legally obliged to choose the most profitable of all available options.

a. Exemption Measure **Business decisions** do not lead to liability if they follow the **Business Judgment Rule**. The application of the Business Judgement Rule should be carefully documented to prevent liability. Also, a shareholder resolution can prevent the personal liability of business managers in a business decision.

b. Business Judgment Rule The **Business Judgment Rule** stipulates that there is no liability-creating breach of duty if business managers could reasonably assume, in a „business decision“, to act for the benefit of the company based on adequate information. To properly exercise the Business Judgement Rule, you should consider the following prerequisites:

- **Appropriate information basis:** Collect and consider sufficient information (this must be documented!)
  - **Avoid:** Unbalanced information basis: Uncomfortable aspects are not even considered
- **Consideration:** Weigh what serves the company's well-being and what harms it (this must be documented!)
  - **Avoid:** Biased evaluation: One-sided focus on desired benefits, irresponsible downplaying of risks
- **Decision:** Choose an action option for the benefit of the company. There will always be an action option, even if this option is to simply do nothing. You should definitely document these different options.
  - **Avoid:** Tunnel vision decisions for „inevitable" or „without alternative"

c. Shareholder resolutions If managing directors act on the basis of a resolution of the shareholders' meeting, they are generally not liable for any damages incurred. This applies even if the action did not correspond to „the diligence of a prudent businessman" *(§ 43 GmbHG)*. Given this far-reaching protection of shareholder resolutions, it is advisable to obtain a shareholder resolution in advance for decisions that will have significant implications for business operations and/or result in significant cash flow. When in doubt, it is better to obtain a shareholder resolution than not to.

However, this protection does not apply if the resolution itself is unlawful and/or not properly concluded.

The following should be considered when passing a shareholder resolution:

- **Clarity:** Shareholder resolution should contain clear, practicable instructions to the management.
- **Preparation of the shareholders:** The shareholders should be properly prepared by providing all relevant information.

- **Legality/no nullity:** Regarding the form and deadline requirements to be observed, you should look at your articles of association and pass the resolution according to these requirements. You should definitely ensure that the resolution is not null and void or contestable.

You should avoid these mistakes when creating shareholder resolutions:

- **No formal resolution:** Informal decisions or statements offer, if at all, only limited protection.
- **Outdated resolution:** Only acting on the basis of a current resolution protects. If the circumstances have already changed after a resolution has been passed, you would need to obtain a new resolution.
- **Partial collection:** For a legally secure resolution, all shareholders must be involved; for example, if only the majority shareholder is asked, there is no resolution of the shareholders' meeting.

2. Legally bound decision The **legally bound decision** must be distinguished from the entrepreneurial decision. A decision is legally bound if there is only **one lawful option** and the decision is limited to „comply with the law or not". **Examples**: Ad-hoc notifications, convening the ordinary shareholders' meeting.

Managing directors must know, understand and choose the lawful option of the applicable laws. If you are not sure whether the law prescribes a decision, you must consult a qualified and independent expert.

Because: Managing directors are generally liable for unlawful decisions. They can exculpate themselves if they have obtained reliable advice (see ISION principles).

Legally bound decisions do not lead to liability if they comply with the ISION principles. Shareholder resolutions can also prevent liability in individual cases for bound decisions, but only if the applicable law does not obviously contradict the resolution or decision.

a. Principles of the ISION Judgment According to the **principles of the ISION judgment** of the BGH, for exoneration it is required that a managing director, if they themselves do not have the necessary expertise, seeks advice from an independent, professionally qualified expert after comprehensive presentation of the company's circumstances and disclosure of the necessary documents, and subjects the legal advice given to a careful plausibility check.

If you want to prevent liability in a bound decision and want to observe the ISION principles, you should pay attention to the following:

- **Expert:** Commissioning of a qualified, independent expert.
- **Non-binding reports:** Do not accept drafts, only final dated reports; observe limitations of the advice (disclaimer of liability!).
- **Provision of all relevant information:** Provision of comprehensive information.

You should definitely **avoid** the following points:

- **No documented factual basis:** The expert must document the scope of the consultation and the relevant factual background.
- **No plausibility check and adoption of the expert opinion:** You must check the advice received for plausibility. Simply adopting the expert's recommendations is not sufficient.
- **Favorable reports:** The report must not be a result-oriented favorable report with biased advice. Therefore, it is important to document a subsequent plausibility check.

3. Documentation is Key Regardless of the type of decision: You must always document that you have taken the exoneration measures. Only through sufficient and proper documentation can a managing director demonstrate in a dispute that they have taken the above-mentioned exoneration measures and thus have not made themselves liable.

The better the documentation, the easier this proof is. Against the background of the reversal of the burden of proof in liability processes, managing directors should set the highest standards for the documentation of their decisions.

The decision-making process and the decision itself can be documented in presentations, decision templates or meeting minutes. Tools like Fides (www.fides.technology) can help you with the correct documentation.

4. Plan B: For Liability: D&O Insurances A D&O insurance stands for „Directors and Officers Insurance“ (also known as „Manager/Organ Liability Insurance“). The D&O insurance is a special type of liability insurance that protects executives such as managing directors from personal liability arising from the decisions and actions in their professional activity.

The D&O insurance provides financial protection for those affected if they are held liable for (alleged) breaches of duty in their function. It covers the costs of legal defense (keyword: „reversal of burden of proof“), claims for damages and other costs associated with liability.

The exact coverage and conditions of a D&O insurance vary greatly depending on the insurance company and contract. It is important to carefully check the insurance conditions and to pay attention to possible exclusions or restrictions. The need for D&O insurance is to be individually coordinated for each company and is based on factors such as legal form, jurisdiction, company size, internationality, stock exchange listing and other individual criteria (e.g. regulated environment, strained financial situation vs. growth company etc.).

It is therefore advisable for managing directors of companies to get a D&O insurance.

Helpful Tools

For most of the above-mentioned administrative tasks, there are already tools that can support you.

a. Fides (www.fides.technology)

Fides is a software that helps you, on the one hand, to observe your corporate legal obligations and, on the other hand, to carry out shareholder resolutions in a lawful manner. Fides also advises on the question of whether you need a shareholder resolution for this business at all. The software then provides the appropriate templates. The entire process of voting and signing the resolution can also be carried out via Fides. The resolution is then properly filed with a legally secure audit trail.

b. Bunch (www.bunch.capital)

Bunch specializes in the trust solution for pooling angels. Bunch thus helps with the management of many pooled angels and acts as a trustee.

© The Author(s), under exclusive license to Springer Fachmedien Wiesbaden GmbH, part of Springer Nature 2025

B. Quarch et al., *Quick Guide Legal Best Practices for Founders in Germany*,
https://doi.org/10.1007/978-3-658-47385-3_8

c. Ledgy (www.ledgy.com) and Carta (www.carta.com)

Cap Table Management Tools like Ledgy and Carta can help you manage your shareholders and VSOPs. Carta is the American solution and Ledgy is the European one. However, this type of tool usually only makes sense when your Cap Table has reached a certain level of complexity due to the issuance of VSOPs or ESOPs.

Protective Rights

The protection of one's own intellectual property (IP) is often not seen as a priority when starting up a start-up. However, for founders, it should be of particular importance to deal not only with the idea and the team, but especially with protective rights in order to protect their intellectual property. Mistakes regarding their IP can usually only be rectified afterwards with great difficulty and then at high cost.

a. Patents

Consequently, you should first check whether your innovation is patentable and consider a potential patent application. It is fundamentally important to know that patents generally protect inventions and grant the holder the exclusive right to use them commercially.

© The Author(s), under exclusive license to Springer Fachmedien Wiesbaden GmbH, part of Springer Nature 2025

B. Quarch et al., *Quick Guide Legal Best Practices for Founders in Germany*,
https://doi.org/10.1007/978-3-658-47385-3_9

b. Trademark

In the next step, you should ensure that the name of your product or service is not already being used elsewhere. Your brand fundamentally characterizes your company and serves to distinguish it from your competition. Publicly accessible online trademark registers are your first port of call. But beware! Within the framework of the register, you can only look for a specific name. Trademarks that also oppose use, such as company identifiers, are not displayed in most cases. Therefore, if your start-up is an international project, it may make sense to hire an external service provider.

After you have chosen the desired name available to you through the trademark search, you need to carry out a trademark application to avoid possible legal problems. An index of goods and services must be attached for the application. Your costs at the German Patent and Trademark Office (DPMA) will continue to amount to a registration fee of 300 € or 290 € for an online application. If you want to register the trademark for more than three goods and service classes, a fee of 100 € will be charged for each additional class. If you are willing to pay an additional 100 € beyond the basic fee, you can have the application examined more quickly.

In addition to words, graphic representations, 3D designs or acoustic identifiers can also be registered and thus protected. Such protection includes not only identical but also confusingly similar signs. However, this protection is not universally valid! It only applies to the country in which the trademark was registered. So if you want to protect your name in several countries, you generally have to apply for a national trademark in each country. You can avoid this by registering a community trademark. This offers protection at least in all EU member states and must be registered with the Office for Harmonization in the Internal Market (OHIM). The online registration of a community trademark with up to three classes costs 900 €. For each additional class, you will be charged 150 €.

After you have done your part for the application, it is initially up to the respective office to check your request. If approved, your application will be published and third parties have the right to object to the registration of your trademark within an objection period. In a final step, the trademark is then entered in the trademark register.

c. Copyright

Copyright protects original works such as software, creative content, design elements or texts from unauthorized use and distribution. In addition to the Design Act and the Patent Act, the Copyright Act (UrhG) is particularly relevant. Therefore, before you use copyrighted content within your company, you should ensure that you already have the necessary rights or acquire the necessary licenses.

The copyright to a work (such as your product) is created in the person who fundamentally created the work (§ 7 UrhG). So if you created your product as a team, all team members are in principle entitled to copyright to the work (§ 8 UrhG), provided that their respective contribution to the work is protectable on its own.

There are also potential dangers in terms of trade secrets. These represent confidential information that, on the one hand, has economic value and, on the other hand, is not generally known. To ensure protection in this regard, you should strive for internal security measures. This can be done, for example, through confidentiality agreements with employees, business contacts and suppliers.

d. Imitation Protection

To ensure imitation protection, it is your task to monitor your products or services and to involve a lawyer or intellectual property expert in case of a potential suspicion of imitation. Please note explicitly that your start-up can never have a copyright and therefore, in principle, has no rights to the product and accordingly cannot take action against third-party users. Such rights must first be acquired from the copyright holders and can be acquired as a simple or exclusive right, as well as spatially, temporally, or with content restrictions. Action against third parties is only possible when the exclusive right of use is transferred. If there is uncertainty about the extent of the granting of usage rights, it is generally assumed in favor of the copyright holder(s) that granted rights should only apply as far as necessary to achieve the contract objective. At this point, the recommendation is to include a clause regarding usage rights in the employment contracts.

Caution is advised if the copyright holder is employed by you. According to § 32a UrhG, they have a claim to appropriate participation if their remuneration is in a conspicuous disproportion to what later comes out of the use of the work in terms of revenues and benefits. Under certain circumstances, therefore, you may face a subsequent payment in case of particular success.

General Terms and Conditions

Let's now address the part of the General Terms and Conditions (GTC). These are essential for successful customer contact. Legally, GTCs find their regulations in the §§ 305 ff. BGB and describe pre-formulated contract conditions for a multitude of contracts, which you can unilaterally impose on your customers when concluding a contract. You can either list such contract conditions in the contract text or completely attach them separately.

GTCs generally lead to a significant strengthening of your legal position and prevent doubts about the contract content due to their contractual regulations. Therefore, GTCs cannot be set up without restrictions. On the one hand, there are some legal requirements that can vary depending on the country in which you operate. In particular, reference should be made to laws regarding consumer protection, e-commerce, copyright, data protection, and advertising. Make sure to adapt your GTCs to applicable regulations. In addition, you must incorporate essential instructions, such as cancellation instructions for distance selling transactions, into your GTCs and avoid non-compliant, thus ineffective clauses. For example, clauses must not be „surprising" and must not disadvantage your counterpart inappropriately in terms

© The Author(s), under exclusive license to Springer Fachmedien Wiesbaden GmbH, part of Springer Nature 2025

B. Quarch et al., *Quick Guide Legal Best Practices for Founders in Germany*,
https://doi.org/10.1007/978-3-658-47385-3_10

of the requirements of good faith. You can only very slightly restrict statutory warranty regulations to the detriment of the other contracting party. The design possibilities in the area of liability for damages are much more generous. Although you are prohibited from limiting your liability under the Product Liability Act or for intent and personal injury, it is possible to limit your liability for all ancillary obligations, breaches of duty by your vicarious agents, and consequential damages due to simple and moderate negligence.

At this point, there is an explicit warning not to simply adopt foreign, unchecked GTCs for your start-up. In most cases, these are warned off, which can then cause delays in the company. You should also make sure to write your GTCs in a user-friendly, i.e., clearly understandable way. Note that GTCs, which are either written on the back of the contract or on a separate document, only become effective against the other contracting party if you expressly and reasonably point out your GTCs before the conclusion of the contract. To counteract later ambiguities or disputes, you should obtain explicit and not tacit consent to your GTCs from your contract partners. Simply put: Put your GTCs on the contract and have it signed. This will undoubtedly give your contract partners' consent to your GTCs.

Also familiarize yourself with the principle of the precedence of individual agreements, which means that your GTCs are displaced by individual agreements with your counterpart. Always write down such agreements explicitly and separately in your contract!

Websites

Let's now turn to the external presentation of your company: the website. Especially in the founding phase, this remains the sole source of information for your customers and investors. Therefore, it should not only be quickly operational and exude seriousness, but also be adaptable to your targeted future growth in a further step.

The creation of such a website requires a high degree of planning, skill, and sensitivity. Be prepared to allocate enough time for the completion of a well-functioning website. Before you worry about your website creator, it is important to create a temporary onepager after the foundation, which you can then gradually expand.

At all times, you should keep your targeted objectives clearly in mind. The early communication of your vision is indispensable for its later success. In this context, ask yourself the following questions: Is your primary goal to offer and promote your products on the website, or should professional information also be provided and leads generated for your customers? Furthermore, you should identify your target group and their needs and interests. This allows you to adapt the content, design, and functionality of your website. In addition, you should

© The Author(s), under exclusive license to Springer Fachmedien Wiesbaden GmbH, part of Springer Nature 2025
B. Quarch et al., *Quick Guide Legal Best Practices for Founders in Germany*, https://doi.org/10.1007/978-3-658-47385-3_11

secure the appropriate domain for your start-up at the beginning of the foundation.

To convey a positive impression of your website, make sure to choose a user-friendly and appealing design and offer clear navigation in the next step. Regarding the content of your website, it is important to create high-quality, diverse, and informative content. Important here is persuasive language and the inclusion of images or possibly videos. Furthermore, it is advisable to carry out search engine optimization so that potential customers can easily access your website. Helpful in this regard are keywords, an optimized page structure, meta tags, and a URL structure. It is essential that you implement technical basics from the beginning to ensure the findability of your website under the start-up name in the Google index.

Especially in the early stages of the foundation, when the first visitors find your website appealing, a newsletter function can be helpful. In this context, you should work with calls to action that go beyond subscribing to your newsletter, such as purchasing your product or filling out a contact form. Speaking of contacts! Make sure that visitors to your website can easily get in touch with you. This can not only be done by providing contact information, the imprint, and a contact form. You can also offer a live chat that assists in answering your customers' questions.

Also, make sure to comply with the legal framework conditions of the respective country. In addition to providing an imprint, there is often an obligation to set up a privacy policy that describes which data can be collected and used and what rights the guests of your website have regarding their data. In case of a violation of these provisions, you face warnings, which you can easily avoid. Furthermore, for your own protection, make sure to make your website secure. The implementation of SSL certificates is recommended to ensure secure data transmission.

To enable an analysis of visitor behavior on your website, especially to gain insights about traffic and conversion rate, it is also advisable to work with an analysis tool. This makes it easier for you to identify areas that need optimization. In particular, conducting A/B tests can help determine which versions of content resonate most with visitors.

Also, expect that your website will require constant adjustments due to feedback from customers, market changes, and technological changes. Only in this way can you meet the needs of your customers and investors.

Founders' Exit

While past generations often dreamed of establishing future-oriented family businesses, many founders today aim to execute a successful exit. This refers to the point in time when you leave the company either by selling the entire company or at least selling your own shares.

A company presentation is indispensable for preliminary discussions with potential buyers. This includes the company's history or development history and a description of the current team. For the sale itself, you should have the articles of association, a financial and business plan, business evaluations, and ongoing customer contracts at hand.

In the context of the sale, it is advisable to involve the legal and financial expertise of third parties who are familiar with company settlements and can design an optimal exit process with you. They can adequately consider your interests in the sales process and include tax and legal aspects in the negotiation and completion of contracts. In this context, you should realize that each exit represents an individual process. Therefore, it should primarily correspond to your personally set goals, needs, and preferences, taking into account the respective circumstances of your start-up. If you are interested in selling certain shares in your company, but still want to remain involved in the company,

© The Author(s), under exclusive license to Springer Fachmedien Wiesbaden GmbH, part of Springer Nature 2025

B. Quarch et al., *Quick Guide Legal Best Practices for Founders in Germany*, https://doi.org/10.1007/978-3-658-47385-3_12

this is referred to as a partial exit. This is particularly considered when you want to access fresh capital. In addition, there are various design options, which can vary depending on the objectives of the founding members and the status of the company.

a. Design Options

Let's now turn to the most common design options or exit strategies. The goal of the exit is, in principle, to at least recover your own investment and, ideally, to exit as profitably as possible, in short: to generate profits and minimize losses.

aa) Acquisition or Complete Sale to Strategic Investors

Successful, innovative start-ups that have an overlapping sphere of influence with a corporation often execute their exit through a complete sale, i.e., the sale including shares and assets, to strategic investors or a large corporation. Note that these initially often only buy shares, but their long-term goal is usually the complete takeover.

bb) Trade Sale and Private Equity

Another exit option is to sell your company to institutional investors who are part of professional investment companies (private equity firms). Private equity firms then seek funds collected in funds to buy shares in companies in a further step. As a result, your company is not taken over in its entirety, and the investors only buy a right to participate and have a say depending on their investment.

cc) Leveraged Buyout (LBO)

If your company already has sufficient financial resources, an exit in the form of a leveraged buyout (debt-financed takeover) could be considered. In this case, investors who have already purchased shares in your company use additional borrowed capital to buy your own shares. To repay the borrowed capital including interest, funds from your company's cash flow are usually used. However, be prepared for the investors buying your shares to subsequently resell these along with their previous shares.

dd) IPO: Going Public

The Rolls Royce among the exit strategies is going public. In technical terms, such a case is referred to as an Initial Public Offering (IPO). Basically, only a few start-ups will manage to exit via the stock exchange. Moreover, it only becomes a final exit once the shares have been sold there. With such an exit strategy, you should therefore expect a much longer implementation time from the outset.

ee) Merger: Exit through Consolidation

Another not unpopular exit-like strategy is the complementary merger with a company that competes with yours. This offers the opportunity to exploit new and innovative market advantages while you hold your shares in the company. With the internal distribution associated with the merger, it may still be possible for you to carry out a partial exit by no longer being financially involved in the company, for example.

ff) Timing

When it makes the most sense for you to plan an exit varies from case to case and depends very much on your motivation behind the company. However, the following generally applies from a strategic point of view: The best time for an exit is usually as soon as your company has a certain size and stability, as you are then most attractive to investors. With the funds you generate in the process, you can then implement and develop new ideas and products in a further step.

b. Typical Contract Components

Even though each takeover contract must be individually drafted, they often contain recurring passages and regulations. Therefore, there are typical components in the context of exits that should be integrated into the respective contracts. You should consider the following list as a checklist for your individually crafted contracts:

- Purchase price and payment modalities
- Warranties or guarantees
- Non-compete clauses
- Restrictions on disposal
- Transition agreements
- Limitations of liability
- Approval requirements and release mechanisms

Please note that contract components and conditions always depend on the parties involved and can therefore vary.

aa) Purchase Price and Payment Modalities

The contract should first contain the purchase price you have agreed with the contract partners for the shares or the entire company. Furthermore, the payment modalities need to be determined. These include, among other things, any down payment amount, possible agreed installment payments, and earn-out arrangements.

bb) Warranties and Guarantees

The contract can also include warranties and guarantees you desire, such as the preservation of intellectual property.

cc) Non-Compete Clauses

Non-compete clauses aim to prohibit the sellers from joining a competitor after a successful exit. The clauses establish regulations about the duration and scope of these competition restrictions. Care should always be taken with the exact wording and scope.

dd) Restrictions on Disposal

In addition, your contract can contain clauses stating that the selling founders are not able to sell their remaining shares immediately after the exit due to buyer protection.

ee) Transition Agreements

Transition provisions are often found in contracts, ensuring necessary transfer measures, such as the obligation of the former founders to cooperate for a certain period or to transfer information.

ff) Limitations of Liability

The contract can also include limitations of liability for founder protection, such as claims for damages or warranties.

gg) Approval Requirements and Release Mechanisms

The contract can also contain clauses about individual approvals or required releases from other people who hold shares or stakes in the company, regulatory authorities, or other relevant internal parties.

Worst-Case Scenario/Exit Strategy/Dispute Among Shareholders

Let's now come to a topic in our final chapter that you hopefully will never have to deal with if you read this book carefully: The worst-case scenario!

In the worst-case scenario, the company is no longer able to manage financial liabilities from its own resources and continue its business operations. Basically, two exit strategies are considered in a worst-case scenario: liquidation and insolvency.

To prevent such crises through early knowledge and timely communication with financing shareholders, it is recommended to make a realistic 13-week short-term and a long-term 14-month liquidity plan. In any case, it is advisable to get extensive advice from people with insolvency and legal expertise for a varying approach from case to case, in order to protect not only your own interests but also the interests of your creditors and co-shareholders. Ideally, a well-thought-out exit strategy for the worst case should already be taken into account in the business plans of the start-up in order to be able to address possible risks and challenges. Early identification of financial problems and the initiation of appropriate measures can help to avoid the worst-case scenario or at least limit the damage.

© The Author(s), under exclusive license to Springer Fachmedien Wiesbaden GmbH, part of Springer Nature 2025

B. Quarch et al., *Quick Guide Legal Best Practices for Founders in Germany*,
https://doi.org/10.1007/978-3-658-47385-3_13

a. Liquidation vs. Insolvency

If your company gets into a financial crisis, there are two basic options to possibly give up or save your start-up's GmbH: Liquidation and insolvency. The procedure is not the same for every type of company and relevant regulations also differ.

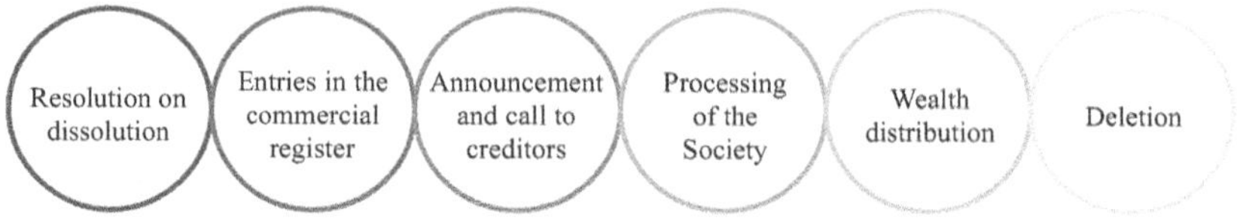

If you have founded your start-up as a GmbH—as is most often the case—the GmbH of the start-up is dissolved in the case of liquidation and its assets or intellectual property are sold off, as the business model of your start-up has failed and there are no longer any prospects of profit. In addition to other reasons for dissolution, the dissolution can be decided by a resolution of the shareholders (§ 60 para. 1 no. 2 GmbHG). It must be registered in the commercial register, as must the liquidators (§ 67 GmbHG), and the dissolution must be announced in the company gazettes. At the same time, the company's creditors are asked to report to the company to settle outstanding debts. The liquidators must wind up ongoing business, collect receivables and convert the assets into cash (§ 70 GmbHG). The resulting funds should be used to settle outstanding liabilities. You do not have to pay your liabilities in a specified order, although higher claim amounts take precedence. The remaining funds, after all debts have been paid, are distributed to you and other shareholders at the earliest after one year, the so-called blocking year (§ 73 GmbHG). Once all the assets of the GmbH have been liquidated and distributed, the termination of the liquidation is entered in the commercial register and the company is deleted (§ 74 GmbHG).

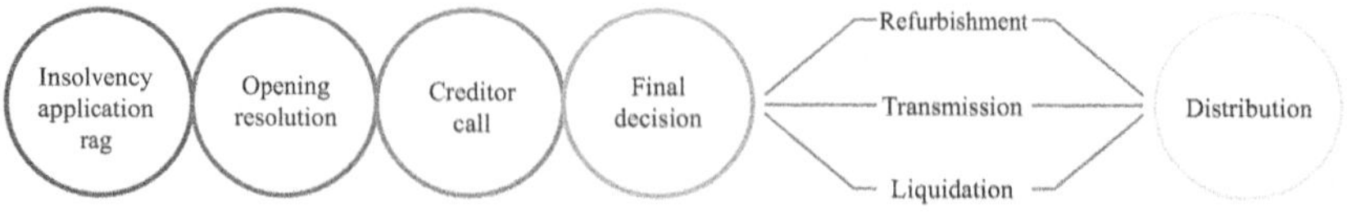

The aim of insolvency, like liquidation, is fundamentally to settle the company's debts. If there is a reason for insolvency (§ 16 InsO)—impending insolvency, insolvency or over-indebtedness (§§ 17, 18, 19 InsO)—an insolvency application can be filed by the creditor or the debtor, i.e., the start-up, which initiates the insolvency proceedings. In case of insolvency or over-indebtedness, the management is obliged to file for insolvency within three or six weeks (§ 15a para. 1 InsO), while such an obligation does not exist in case of impending insolvency and is voluntarily initiated by the founders. A preliminary insolvency proceeding begins, in which it is checked whether there is a reason for insolvency and whether there is enough assets to carry out the insolvency proceedings. If there are not enough assets to cover the costs of the insolvency proceedings, the insolvency application will be rejected due to lack of assets (§ 26 InsO). Otherwise, the proceedings are opened, an insolvency administrator is appointed (§ 27 InsO) and the opening is announced. In the opening decision, the creditors of your company are called upon to register their claims, which are included in the insolvency table. The insolvency administrator takes control of your company and checks whether it should be dissolved or whether the company can still be restructured. He informs the creditors' meeting about the financial situation of the company and potential restructuring options (§ 156 InsO). They decide on the further course of the proceedings: the cessation or the provisional continuation and possibly the creation of a comprehensive insolvency plan (§ 157 InsO). If no continuation is decided, the realization of the debtor's assets begins (§ 159 InsO). Depending on the financial situation, a likely strategy is the complete sale of the company to another company or other investors. It is also possible to sell to already involved shareholders. Otherwise, the assets, the insolvency estate, are liquidated to satisfy the creditors. After their claims have been examined by the insolvency administrator, the claims are divided into special groups and put in a corresponding order, as some creditors have to be satisfied first. Afterwards, a quota is formed, according to which the creditors are proportionally satisfied from the insolvency estate.

Under certain circumstances, the managing directors may be forced to initiate insolvency proceedings. The opening of the insolvency proceedings, like a corresponding shareholders' resolution, constitutes a reason for dissolving the GmbH (§ 60 para. 1 no. 4 GmbHG). Often, for the purpose of damage limitation, it may be sensible for you not to wait for insolvency, but to prepare for liquidation in good time and to initiate it independently by resolution. In contrast to liquidation, your company is considered insolvent in the event of insolvency. If the management does not file a mandatory insolvency application, its members are liable to prosecution. As a result, they may be deprived of the right to hold the position of managing director for the following five years. On the other hand, insolvency can be a stimulus for a fundamental restructuring that can allow your start-up to grow sustainably again. Liquidity aids such as insolvency money support the restructuring.

b. Liability Risks in Insolvency

Caution is advised even before insolvency! Managing directors are liable for tax debts that they have culpably failed to pay (§ 34, 69 AO). In connection with insolvency, however, there are some additional, specific civil and criminal liability pitfalls that you should familiarize yourself with.

In the event of insolvency itself, the opening of the proceedings, as already mentioned, usually depends on the filing of the application. The insolvency application must be filed immediately, at the latest after three or six weeks, regardless of the subjective knowledge of the managing directors. Simple negligence of the deadline suffices in this case! In addition, there is a presumption rule regarding the fault of the managing directors. This means: In a serious case, you must prove that despite sufficient organizational precautions, you could not have known about the circumstances and took all reasonable measures to fulfill your application obligation. If the management does not comply with the application obligation, criminal liability for insolvency delay according to § 15a para. 4 InsO is possible. Other insolvency offenses include bankruptcy (§§ 283, 283a StGB), violation of the accounting obligation (§ 283b StGB) and creditor and debtor favoritism (§§ 283 c, 283 d StGB) as well as fraud (§ 263 StGB) or embezzlement of wages (§ 266a para. 1 StGB) in the event of intentional violation of the obligation to pay social security contributions. If you, as a managing director, make false statements, you could also be liable under § 82 para. 2 GmbHG.

In addition, a reduction in the insolvency assets available to satisfy creditors usually results in damage to other parties. New contracts would not be concluded in most cases if the financial situation of the company was known. Because of your general duties of loyalty and care (§ 43 para. 2 GmbHG) towards the GmbH, you are therefore liable if the insolvency application is negligently delayed or not filed at all. The management is liable for these damages to the contractual partners of the company also under § 823 para. 2 BGB in conjunction with § 15a para. 4 InsO and other criminal offenses. In the same way, personal liability of managing directors and other persons who knew about the insolvency can be established under § 826 BGB. After the occurrence of insolvency or the determination of over-indebtedness, payments from the GmbH's assets may generally not be made, unless this is compatible with the care of a prudent and conscientious business manager (§ 15b para. 1 InsO). A violation can lead to liability under § 15b para. 4 InsO. In addition, you have the duty to set aside necessary funds in time to be able to use them when liabilities become due. In a serious case, this can lead to wage cuts for your staff. Keep in mind that even with reduced wages, employee contributions to social security must be paid properly.

c. Dispute among the Shareholders

The worst case scenario among founders, of course, is the—not so rare—case of dispute. It often happens that the founders develop in different directions or develop different interests. The convertible loan is mentioned as an example: Some founders favor taking out high loans. Others prefer to put fewer shares into the ring. If the founders are at odds and no one is willing to take over the other's shares according to their ideas (this is particularly relevant when there is already a significant valuation), the only way is through a forced separation.

Depending on the design of the partnership agreement, it is necessary to withdraw shares from other shareholders or to exclude them. In both cases, a valid reason is necessary. The differentiation between the withdrawal and the exclusion (or a combination of both) is important. In the case of a withdrawal—which must be explicitly anchored in the partnership agreement—the person who may have realized the important reasons has no voting rights in the decision about the withdrawal. He must then sue within a specified period (usually one month) against the effectiveness of the resolution. The remaining shareholders must then present and prove the important reasons. However, the withdrawal takes effect immediately and the managing directors have the opportunity to adjust the shareholder list. Although there are legal remedies for the affected shareholder, these are complex and should be coordinated with a legal expert. If a withdrawal is not possible, the shareholder can be excluded. Unlike the withdrawal, the company must have the effectiveness of the exclusion determined by a court. Depending on the design of the partnership agreement, the affected shareholder remains a shareholder for as long as it is established that there are important reasons. Most partnership agreements provide for two options: Either the share expires or another shareholder takes over the shares. This determines who has to pay the compensation due to the departing shareholder. The amount of the compensation depends on the valuation. As a rule, the departing shareholder must demonstrate the amount of his/her claim. The mechanisms that are conceivable in the event of a dispute, such as in a game of chess, must be planned in advance. A good strategy leads to the goal here.

The manufacturer's authorised representative in the EU is Springer Nature Customer Service Centre GmbH, Europaplatz 3, 69115 Heidelberg, Germany. If you have any concerns regarding our products, please contact ProductSafety@springernature.com

Printed and bound by CPI Group (UK) Ltd, Croydon, CR0 4YY
30/09/2026
02225606-0001